YANNIS DESYPRIS

KARPATHOS
& KASSOS

a folklore paradise

EDITIONS
TOUBI'S®
ΕΚΔΟΣΕΙΣ
ATHENS 2001

Texts: YANNIS DESYPRIS
Text supervision: DAPHNE CHRISTOU
Artistic supervision: EVI DAMIRI
Translation: JUDY GIANNAKOPOULOU
Photographs: MICHALIS TOUBIS S.A. FILES

Colour separations, printing: M.TOUBIS GRAPHIC ARTS S.A.

Copyright © 2001 M. TOUBIS EDITIONS S.A. 519 Vouliagmenis Ave., Ilioupoli, Athens GR-163 41 GREECE.
Tel. (301) 9923876, Fax: (301) 9923867
NTERNET: http://www.toubis.gr
ISBN: 960-540-411-7

«Karpathos, lovely island, with fairest winds,
You're ever cool, both winter and summer.
Karpathos, with your twelve pretty villages
that bore your good children, your pride and your joy:
Pigadia, Arkassa, Menetes, Volada and Aperi
Othos, Piles and Olympos, Spoa and Misohori,
Yiafani and my Finiki and beautiful coastlines,
fountains of cold water, running like crystal».

Folk song

Contents

Kyra-Panayia.

1 KARPATHOS

It may not be an exaggeration to say that Karpathos is the richest place in all Greece in terms of living folklore; it is the place that has kept up its customs and manners better than any other. This can be experienced in the most striking way. We enjoy it at the festivals in the famous village of Olympos, when all the women wear their colourful traditional dresses with the double row of gold coins round their necks and pretty kerchiefs on their heads. We can confirm it when we visit a traditional house and see the typical arrangement of its interior, with its rare textiles and embroideries: a house that could easily be described as a tiny museum.

But it isn't just the tradition and folklore that make Karpathos different. It is also the superb landscape: high mountains that descend in steep cliffs to lacy coastlines of dazzling white sand. The famous Kyra-Panayia, Ahata and Apella are just three of the delightful beaches showing off the deep blue of the sea. On its pine-clad mountains, picturesque villages look snow white; while nestled in leeward coves are settlements and resorts, large and small, that attract visitors during the summer.

The second-largest island in the Dodecanese, Karpathos has seen its population seriously depleted by migration, although now things have changed. The migrants are coming back and the seaside summer resorts are growing. Every year, more and more visitors want to become acquainted with this island which was virgin territory until very recently. Its international airport, hotels, improved roads –at least in the southern part of the island– and the hospitality of the local people guarantee visitors comfortable, unforgettable holidays.

a folklore paradise

Geography: Together with the smaller island of Kassos, Karpathos is the southernmost island in the Dodecanese. It is situated between Crete and Rhodes and is the second largest island in the group, with an area of 301 km^2. The length of its coastline is 160 km. and it has a population of 6500 inhabitants.

Morphology: Karpathos is an island 49 km. long, with a maximum width of 11 km. and a minimum -in about the middle of the island- of just 3.3 km. Its highest mountain is Kali Limni, which rises to an altitude of 1215 m. Other peaks are Profitis Ilias (1168 m.) and Lastos (975 m.) in the centre of the island, and Profitis Ilias (718 m.) near Olympos, in the northern part of the island. A channel no more than 200 m. wide separates Karpathos from the rocky but interesting islet of Saria, which which Karpathos was once united. Saria has an area of 19 km^2 and is 8 km. long.

Local products: The main products of Karpathos are the grapes that produce high quality wine, as well as olive oil, cheese, honey, oranges, lemons, quinces, apples, etc. Among the island's products must be included its traditional folk art items such as Karpathian plates, woven goods and copper utensils.

KARPATHOS

LEGEND

Pavod road	
Non-paved road	
Poor road	
Church	

Archaeological site

Cave

Beach

Airport

N

NISSYROS

SARIA

FRASSONISID

Agios Ioannis
VRYKOUS
Avlona

Diafani

Olympos

Agios Nikolaos
718

Fyses

Limeri

Forokli

Vananaa

Agios Minas

692

Mesohori

Spoa

Agios Nikolaos

Apela

Apela

1168

Agios Georgios

Archagellos Michail

1215

Kyra Panagia

Lefkos

Mertonas
Katodio

Anaca

Agia Kyriaki

Agios Panteleimon

Volada
Agios Georgios

Aperi
Profitis Ilias

Troplama

Stes
Othos

Agios Nikolaos

KOURI

Piles

Agios Nektarios

Karpathos
Larniotissa

685

POTIDAION

Agia Kyriaki

Finiki
Agios Mamas

Menetes

Profitis Elias

Lakki

Amor

Arkasa

Agios Nikolaos

ARKESIA

MIRA

Agios Ioannis

FRASSONISID

Geology

There are many different geological formations on the island. In the southern part we encounter laminated limestones. In the central and southern parts of the island there are reef limestones and bitumenous dolomites as well as flysch with intrusions of gypsum. Marls and marly sandstones are found between Kastello Bay, Arkassa and Pano Aphiartis.

The natural environment

The visitor's first impression of Karpathos is of a bare, rocky island with no forests. The fact is that Karpathos is a botanical and zoological paradise, with many rare, even unique species of plants and animals.

The dense pine forest in central Karpathos -particularly in the region of Piles, Mesohori and Spoa- its vineyards and plentiful fruit trees provide visitors with the first evidence of the island's abundant natural environment.

Regarding flora in particular, the following plants are endemic to the island: Silene insularis, Erysimum candicum ssp. carpathum, Ricotia isatoides, Limonium carpathum, Origanum vetteri, Carthamus rechingeri and Ophrys aegaea.

Other rare plants on Karpathos, endemic to the southern or southeastern Aegean, are Hypericum cuisinii, Paeonia clusii, Limonium fredericii, Teucrium heloiotropifolium, Campanula carpatha, Dianthus fruticosus ssp. carpathus, Trifolium praetermissum, Nigelia carpatha, Campanula panatzii, Phlomis pichleri, Silene ammophila ssp. carpatha, Bellis longifolia, Astragalus austroaegaeus, Limonium pigadiense, Ranunculus cupreus, Anemone heldreichii, etc. Mention should also be made of species that are rare or unique in Europe, such as Phlomis floccosa, Crocus biflorus ssp. nubigena and Silene macrodonta, as well as some which, although not particularly rare, are strikingly beautiful, such as Ranunculus asiaticus and Tulipa saxatilis.

The island is similarly rich in fauna. The Mediterranean monk seal (Monachus monachus) finds shelter in the sea caves on the

4 *coast. The seaside rocks also provide a nesting place for the black falcon (*Falco eleonorae*) and the wild gull (*Larus audouinii*), two protected species. Most of the world's population of these birds is found in the Aegean.*

Many migratory birds come to rest on Karpathos on their long voyage across the sea. They include bee-eaters, rollers, various species of swallows, turtle doves, nuthatches, storks, golden eagles, etc. And finally we should mention the island's unique amphibian Mertensiella luscani, *which has adapted to the dry climate and survives in summer by hiding under damp rocks or in cool dry riverbeds. This species exists only on the islands of Karpathos and Kastellorizo.*

1. Paeonia clusii, *endemic to Karpathos.*
2. Lotus cytisoides; *found on Saria and Karpathos.*
3. Anchusa aegyptica.
4, 5. *Scenes near Othos.*

MYTH AND HISTORY

Mythology

Karpathos, with its high, forested mountains and verdant gullies, appears to have fascinated the ancient Hellenes. This may be why, in Greek mythology, it is regarded as being the home of many significant mythical creatures. According to one version of the story, the first inhabitant of Karpathos was the Titan Iapetus, son of U-ranus and Gaea and brother of Cronus, the father of Zeus. Another version has all Titans living together on the island, prior to the famous Battle of the Titans described to us by Hesiod, during which the Titans who were gathered on the Othris peak were defeated by Zeus and the twelve gods from Mt Olympus in Thessaly.

But Karpathos did not play host solely to the Titans; it also provided a home to the Giants who were likewise children of Gaea's. Among them was Ephialtes, Otus' twin brother. The name Aphiartis, a well-known site in the southern part of the island, appears to be a corruption of the word Ephialtes, and is seen to provide evidence of this link. In addition, Iapetus' son Prometheus, who stole fire from Zeus to give it to man, also lived on the island. What the myths do not specify is whether Zeus, in order to avenge himself on Prometheus, sent Pandora and her box to Karpathos or found him in some other place.

And finally, it is likely that the Telchines, cele-

*Above: Ruins in Paleokastro.
Opposite: Ruins of basilica
of Ayia Fotini in Pigadia.*

brated metalworkers who according to tradition were the first to process copper and iron, came during the prehistoric years from the coast of Asia Minor to settle on Karpathos. Some regard them as mythical creatures, others as common mortals.

Regarding the name of the island, there are a number of different versions, none of which can be documented. One of them links the name of the island with the plant carpaso that used to be grown on Karpathos. The same plant also gave its name to the town of Karpassia on Cyprus, where it was also grown.

Pre-historic period

The theory that the first inhabitants of Karpathos were Minoans appears to have been disproved after the discovery of finds, mainly in caves, indicating that the island was inhabited for the first time in the Neolithic period. There is of course no doubt that the influence of neighboring Minoan Crete was strong, and that Potidaio, present-day Pigadia, was colonised by the Minoans. The oldest findings from the acropolis or citadel of Potidaio and from Paleokastro -the acropolis of ancient Arkesia, near today's Arkassa- date back to about 2500 BC. The influence of the Minoans began to be visible around 1600 BC.

The Myceneans made their appearance in the 14th century BC, by conquering the island and repairing the walls of the Potidaio acropolis. Their stay on Karpathos can be demonstrated by the large number of Mycenean vessels found there.

And speaking of the Myceneans, it should be noted that Homer, who calls the island Krapathos, relates in the Iliad that Krapathos sent ships to participate in the Trojan War. Traces of the Phoenicians have also been found on the island. They were a seafaring people whose ships were then sailing around the Mediterranean carrying their products to a number of different countries, developing trade and establishing trading posts on the islands and coasts of Greece. On Karpathos, however, their activities extended to another realm: they gathered the Murex mollusc from which they extracted the Tyrian purple used to dye their famous textiles. Owing to this fact, Karpathos during that period was also called Porphyris (=purple) by the Phoenicians. In addition, it should be noted here that the name of a harbour on the western coast of the island, which today is a tourist resort named Finiki, contains echoes of the presence of Phoenicians on the island. After the Myceneans and Phoenicians, the Dorians came to the island in about 1000 BC.

Historic period

The Dorians brought the greatest prosperity to the island. During their era, Karpathos was also called Tetrapolis, owing to its four prosperous, fortified towns. These towns were Potidaio, or Poseidio which is present-day Pigadia; Arkesia or Arkeseia, near today's tourist village of Arkassa with its famous acropolis; Vrykous on the northern tip of the island, where ruins can still be seen of buildings and especially parts of walls; and Nisyros, situated on what is today the rocky islet of Saria north of Karpathos. The discovery of iron and silver mines on the island may have contributed to the prosperity of these towns.

Karpathos was part of the first Delian League in 478 BC. This was why the island was an ally of Athens in the Peloponnesian War (431-404 BC). But after Athens was defeated in 404 BC, it came under the Spartans, to be reoccupied in 397 BC by the Athenians, then led by the admiral Conon. After this victory, the Athenians gave the island autonomy.

In the Hellenistic period, Karpathos was subject to the neighbouring, powerful Rhodes.

1. The archaeological site at Potidaio.　　　　*2. Icon screen from the church of the Dormition of the Virgin.*

The Roman and Byzantine period

In the middle of the 1st century AD, Karpathos was conquered by the Romans and during the reign of the emperor Diocletian (245-313 AD) became part of the so-called Province of the Islands.

Long before Diocletian, the Roman general Lucullus had lived there, a man celebrated for his love of good food. It is said that the general sent a special ship to Karpathos to catch parrot fish, the delicacy found in abundance in the island's waters, and bring the catch to Italy for his banquets. In 330 AD, Constantine the Great selected Constantinople as the new capital of the Roman Empire and legalised Christianity. But the Byzantine period did not begin in essence until 395 AD when the emperor Theodosius I divided the Roman Empire into Eastern and Western. To the former, i.e. the Eastern empire, belonged Karpathos, which was eventually annexed to the theme of Crete.

A few years earlier (in 391 AD), the same emperor had declared Christianity to be the official state religion. That was when the first Christian churches began to be built.

Karpathos was soon taking part in this activity, and many early Christian basilicas were built on the island, such as that of Ayia Fotini near Pigadia, Ayia Anastasia in Paleokastro, and others.

The 5th century AD was characterised by the successive raids and plundering of Karpathos's coastal settlements and especially Pigadia, by Arabs, Saracens, Mauritanians and other pirates. This fact obliged the inhabitants of these regions to seek refuge in the mountains. Thus the villages of Aperi, Volada, Othos, Menetes and Olympos were created, while Pigadia eventually became a pirates' lair.

2

The periods of Latin and Turkish rule

Immediately after the sack of Constantinople by the soldiers of the 4th Crusade in 1204, the government of Karpathos was taken over by Leon Gavalas, scion of an old noble family of Constantinople, who at the same time ruled Rhodes and a few other islands. Gavalas, who was also known as the «lord of the Cyclades», ruled the island until 1224, when he was succeeded by his brother Ioannis.

From 1282 to 1306, the lords of Karpathos were the brothers Andrea and Luigi Moresco from Genoa. Throughout the period of Latin rule, the island was known by the Italian name of Scarpanto.

After the Genoans, the Venetians held sway on Karpathos. In 1306, the island was captured by Andrea Cornaro, who was descended from a powerful old Venetian family. In 1311, Cornaro's rule was interrupted by the Knights of Rhodes who occupied the island until 1315 when the Venetian prince recaptured it. During the Cornaro period, fortresses and many churches were built.

The Cornaro family remained in power until 1537, when the notorious pirate Barbarossa plundered Karpathos, and then handed it over to the Turks who were never particularly interested in it. On the contrary, it could even be said that they avoided it, as very few Turks took up permanent residence there. Of course they sent a judge and a clerk, who remained there for as long as was necessary and immediately afterwards returned home. This is why very little on Karpathos today reminds us of the Turkish presence. Perhaps the Turks avoided the island because of the strong presence of pirates there. Because there is no doubt that Karpathos had become a hive of piracy and that Arkesia even had a slave market operating on their behalf.

1

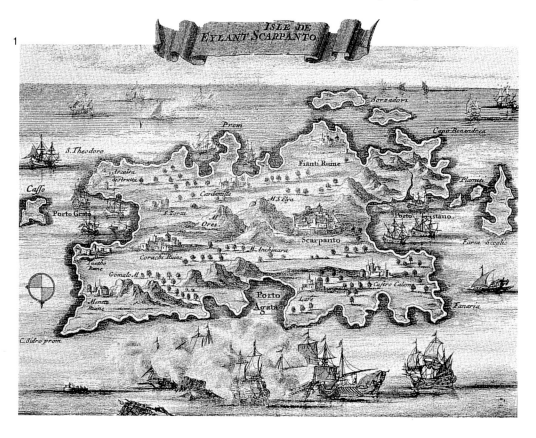

Modern times

As the centuries passed, the fear of pirates frequently disturbed the peace and quiet of the inhabitants, obliging them to move up to the mountainous parts of the island. The Turks, despite their absence, remained the silent but undisputed lords of the island. And then the time came for the great uprising. In April 1821, within just a month after the War of Independence was declared in the Peloponnese, most of the islands of the Dodecanese, including Karpathos, had raised the banner of the Revolution. In the case of Karpathos, it started on 25 April 1821 when a ship's captain from Kassos came to the island with a number of ships and stirred up the local people. From then on, Karpathos offered a great deal to the struggle, primarily funds and supplies. The hospitable Karpathian coasts and particularly the port of Tristomo often provided shelter for fighting Greek ships. There were even shipyards in the bay of Kyra Panayia. The battle was fierce and liberation finally came in 1823. The island was then united with free Greece and became part of the Province of Santorini.

But the joy of freedom was short-lived because in 1830, under the Protocol of London, the Dodecanese was given back to Turkey, and in 1912, was captured by the Italians. Even though the Italians were more interested in Rhodes, they did not fail to leave their traces on Karpathos, as on the other islands. The Italian Command on Karpathos was built on a high rocky coast on the western tip of the port in Pigadia, and serves today as the Eparchio, the Regional Records Office.

Karpathos, like all of Greece, went through a painful period in World War II. German troops arrived on the island in 1943 to join up with the Italians in the war against the Allies. The Germans, who were losing the battle on other fronts, withdrew from Greece on 4 October 1944. The Italians remained. But the Karpathians were no longer willing to put up with foreign occupation. The uprising against their oppressors of 32 years started on 5 October 1944 from the village of Menetes. The men of the village got out their hidden guns and turned them against the Italians. From the very first day, the inhabitants of the village of Arkassa sided with them. In three days, the island of Karpathos was free. The villages of Mesohori and Olympos remained under Italian occupation but they too were liberated on 12 October. But the allies failed to arrive, and the following winter found the island isolated, with its inhabitants facing the grim spectre of starvation. Then seven brave young men set out from Finiki in a small caique, and after five days at sea, managed to reach Alexandria to ask for the intervention of the Greek government in exile. They returned on 17 October 1944 with two allied destroyers; only then was the official liberation of the island celebrated. The Dodecanese, including Karpathos, remained for a few years under the suzerainty of the British (until 7 March 1948), at which time they were united with the rest of Greece.

1. Engraving calling Karpathos by its Italian name of Scarpanto.
2. The Records Office (Eparchio) in Pigadia dates from the period of Venetian rule on the island.

3

CULTURE AND TRADITION

People and occupations

Karpathos is very close to Crete, and so it is natural that its inhabitants, most of whom originate from Crete, have many traits in common with their neighbours. Indeed, the pride, gallantry, commitment to tradition and hospitality that are characteristic of the Cretans are traits frequently found among the Karpathians. This similarity, visible at all times, becomes even more obvious in regard to manners and customs, and in particular in their festivities, as we

Sometimes you feel that time stands still on Karpathos.

under harsh conditions forged the inhabitants' tough, rugged character, which was more or less acquired by the other Karpathians as well. But at the same time it brought great virtues: industriousness, solidarity and love of progress.

Having said these few words about the inhabitants of Karpathos, let us turn to their occupations. The variety of the Karpathian terrain and the climatic conditions in the region have made it relatively suitable both for farming and stock-breeding. In the mountains with their

shall see later. There we'll observe the ease with which the lyre player can compose the famous couplets in which the Karpathians express their feelings, exactly as the Cretans do, and we'll be able to see how closely related their songs and dances are to those of Crete.

But it isn't just the proximity to Crete that has shaped the character and temperament of the Karpathians. Equally important is the influence of the island's natural environment. This of course chiefly applies to the mountainous, northern section of Karpathos, with its mountains and largely barren terrain. There the struggle to survive

scrubby vegetation, it is easy for goats and sheep to find food; while in the fertile gullies, on the plateaus and especially on the lowlands in the southern part of the island, cereals thrive (wheat, barley, corn, rye), as do pulses (beans, lentils, peas etc.), vegetables, vines, olive and fruit trees.

In fact, just a few years ago, the economy of Karpathos relied on revenues from farming, stock-breeding and forestry (today it is forbidden to log these forests) and the primary occupations of the inhabitants were in these fields as technicians (builders, blacksmiths, quarrymen) and in the coastal regions as seamen and merchants.

The local people grazed their flocks on the mountains, sowed wheat and barley, reaped it, threshed it and carried the seeds to the windmills or watermills to be ground into the flour their wives used to make bread. The wives would help the men with their chores as much as they could, as well as cooking, looking after the children, and weaving all the family clothing on the loom.

But farming is arduous, demanding work, especially for the inhabitants of the mountain villages, and frequently had uncertain results, a fact that cultivated gradually, as it did throughout all of Greece, the idea of migrating to seek a better life. Many people went to America; others moved to different parts of Greece.

Old-time occupations are kept up with affection in a town that respects tradition.

relatives who remained there, as well as the island itself. The only problem is that the houses they build now are modern and no longer conform to the traditional architecture (especially in Pigadia). Tourist development, on the other hand, is gradually creating new occupations, the purpose of which is to serve tourists. The number of shops, restaurants, and cafes in Pigadia is increasing, as is the number of hotels and rooms to rent. The same is true of other seaside regions that are being developed. Life on Karpathos, after the decline brought about by migration, is not only getting back into step, but is going ahead with new and favorable prospects.

Above: Picturesque seaside scenes.
The sign dia Xeiros *proclaims that goods are handmade, whether in a shop (below) or outdoors (opposite).*

The countryside was abandoned and thousands of stremmas of arable land were left untilled. Windmills no longer ground wheat and barley into flour, but fell into disrepair. Flour is now brought in from off the island and the ovens that were es-sential for every house, are no longer used. Only in Olympos, the village where time has stood still, do you find looms in use. You will also find one or two windmills turning, reminding us of the old days, and a shoemaker who still manufactures the traditional local boots or stivania.

Migration did not change the way of life alone; it also resulted in reducing significantly the number of farmers and even more so the number of shepherds. Bee-keeping alone showed some improvement as old hives were replaced with hives of a new type. The craft industry of pottery flourished somewhat, obviously due to increased tourism. These migrants have now become new visitors to Karpathos. Most of them have already made enough money to build a new house on the island and to help their

Manners and customs

It might have been possible for tourist development and the new way of life that has already made its presence felt on the island to have had an adverse effect on efforts to preserve the traditional manners and customs. Oddly enough, not only have these efforts not been diminished by tourism, but on the contrary, as a reaction to the changes that have taken place, Karpathians have strengthened their faith and have shown once more their dedication to preserving their manners and customs, which they are very proud of. The only thing they ask is an opportunity to prove it, which is given to them on every feastday, at every festival when, as well as celebrating themselves, they invite visitors to come and celebrate with them. Visitors, who may feel somewhat embarrassed or shy at the beginning, soon take heart and celebrate with the local people in a truly unforgettable experience. And if they are lucky enough for this festivity to be held in traditional Olympos, then they will be enjoying the colourful traditional dress that almost all the women of Olympos wear on feastdays.

Local dress: one of the most characteristic folklore elements on the island. The «sakkofoustano» (jacket-skirt, the costume worn by unmarried women) is in two parts and is divided in the centre. The upper part (the sakko) stops at the waist and is decorated with pleats and cords. The exquisite fousta reaches down to the calves and is made from material of either many colours or a single colour. The apron (podia) is also of many colours and is about the same length as the skirt, i.e. short enough to show off the woven red stockings and elegant slippers made by local shoemakers. Two rows of gold coins are hung around the neck covering virtually the entire chest, and the costume is supplemented by a pretty embroidered head kerchief. This is the official festive outfit. The daily garments are simpler. Instead of a sakofoustano, they wear a kavaï (the costume worn by older women), a type of dark-coloured jacket with garlands on the collar and sleeves (under the «kavai» they wear a white tunic with embroidery in many colours). An apron is essential here, but it is simple, and instead of wearing the traditional boots or stivania on their feet, they wear the type of boot that is required for working in the fields. In the old days, the men of Olympos also wore the traditional dress, which included baggy blue trousers (vraka) and a blue double-breasted vest, all woven in the village. This ensemble was supplemented by a red fez for the elders and a high cap for the others. Needless to say, these garments have changed with the passage of time and differ from one village to another.

The main events in the life of the Karpathians are weddings, baptisms, feastdays and festivals, when music, singing and dancing play a significant role.

Weddings

A Karpathian man's wedding is perhaps the happiest event in his life. So naturally, he and his relatives will celebrate it as well as possible. U-sually the entire village celebrates with him.

The entire wedding process, which lasts more than a week, differs slightly from one place to ano-ther, especially comparing the villages of Lower Karpathos with those of Upper Karpathos, i.e. Mesohori and Olympos. Nevertheless, the basic principles of the customs we shall be describing here remain the same, for both rich and poor. The old custom whereby the family's first-born child, whether it was a son (kanakaris) or daughter (kanakara), used to inherit the entire family fortune has been abolished by law so that this disparity between siblings has now ceased to exist.

Weddings in Karpathos were usually arranged. In such cases, the matchmakers had the last word, as they subtly tried to obtain the consent of the parents. This is why their visits would usually take place in the evening. In any event, the last word belonged to the parents and close relatives:

«When I was two years old and you were four,
your mother promised I would marry you.»

When the agreement was reached between the parents of the groom and the bride, the relatives were informed and then, either the very same day or the next, they would gather at the bride's house. Among them of course was the groom, who would be served some treat in front of the bride and would then put gold coins on the tray according to what his financial situation permitted. In-laws would give gifts to both the groom and the bride. Then they would all sit at the table and take part in a festive meal with lyres and lutes, where the required good wishes would be made:

«Best wishes for a happy, golden, blessed time,
and may the ring you put on be solid.»

This was the brief engagement, unless the bride and groom wanted an official engagement and had time for it.

Many of these customs have been preserved up to the present time. The wedding would normally take place a week after the engagement, and almost always on Sunday. Within the intervening week, all the preparations had to be made. The village, which participated as a whole, would become a hive of activity. From the previous Sunday, the dressmakers would start making the wedding dress. Then the house would be whitewashed, the girls would make the bread including the special round wedding bread, called psilokouloura. There are special songs about the psilokouloura.

«Girls, shape the braided strands of the koulouria prettily
and wish the couple a happy life for a thousand years.»

On Friday is the decoration of the house in which the couple will live, and on Saturday the xylaes will carry the wood (xylo) to cook the food, and the kalestres will walk around the village inviting (kalo) friends and relatives to the wedding.

Then Sunday, the great day, arrives. In the morning, the food will start being cooked and a few hours before the wedding, the last call will go out for the stefanosi, or «crowning with wreaths», which is part of the Greek wedding ceremony. If the wedding is taking place in a mountain village, guests from other villages will have arrived by car or mule. The picture of the animals decorated with colourful blankets is always a popular theme for folklore lovers. With the last call begins the dressing of the bride and groom by the young women and men. Here too, is an opportunity to express good wishes.

«Let this be a good time for your beginning and
let the Virgin Mary and Christ be with you, my child.»

The groom, accompanied by the best man and his friends, sets out to get the bride from her house, so that they can go to the church together (in Mesohori, the groom and bride go to the church separately). At the head of the procession are musicians playing the lyre, the lute and the tsabouna. They arrive at the church and the ceremony begins, after which it is customary for the guests to kiss the newly married couple and their wreaths, placing their gifts on a tray. From the church, the newlyweds will go to their house where the groom will break a red pomegranate, to ensure that their life together is «rosy», and as a symbol of fertility, and then they proceed to the place where the bridal banquet is to be held. There the feasting goes on till the wee hours, with dancing and singing among which will be heard the Karpathian rhyming couplets:

«Who made the match and took such measures
and brought gold together with diamond treasures?
Oh groom, to wed the only daughter you deserve,
and from this day on, your house you will preserve.»

The party continues on the second day, and on the following Sunday will be celebrated the «anti-wedding» or «wedding week».

«Baptisms» and «Efta»

Having spoken about weddings, we should now say a few words about the **efta** (=seven), a custom that takes place seven days after the birth of a child. Friends and relatives then gather together with their gifts, without any special invitation, to offer their good wishes to the newborn baby in its kounia or little hammock. If there is no kounia, then a makeshift one is made of blankets by the young girls in the village. They place the baby in it and rock it, singing couplets that sometimes take the form of wishes and at others are lullabies.

«Come Fates dressed in gold on the Efta
his throne to chart with diamond pens
Come Sleep and get him. Lull him, Sleep.
If there are apples cut them and feed him biscuits.»

Visitors are offered a sweet called alevras made of flour, butter and honey. A party usually follows.

At **baptisms** or christenings, which take place later, relatives are invited in particular, and friends as well. After the church ceremony, everybody gathers in the home of the parents of the child who has just been baptised, where the godfather will hand the child over to its mother and will give some money to its parents, brothers and sisters, and of course, something better (usually gold) to the godchild. A meal will follow with traditional makarounes (homemade pasta) and, as always, a party with traditional dances and songs.

«I am wondering how to start
and how to end
and to the newly baptised,
I'll make many wishes.
Like a stone firmly set,
may the name take root
and to the godfather and parents
much joy may he/she give.»

Typical baby's hammock
from the Folklore Museum.

29

Feastdays and cultural events

The various feastdays, festivals and cultural events on the island provide a wonderful opportunity to enjoy a traditional island festivity. Briefly, the most important and most interesting feastdays are:

- 2 February, feast of the Presentation of the Virgin, in Arkassa
- 23 April, feast of St George, in Lefko
- 5 May, feast of St Irene, at the church of Ayia Irini in Mesohori
- 7 July, feast of St Kyriaki, at Ayia Kyriaki near Pigada
- 26-28 July, feast of St Panteleimon at Othos
- 5-6 August, feast of the Christ the Saviour at Menetes and Diafani.
- 10 August, feast of Chrysovalandos at Olympos (the second most important feast in the village)
- 15 August, the Dormition of the Virgin, in Olympos (the most important festival in the village), at Menetes, Aperi, Pyles.

- 23 August, feast of the Virgin Mary, at Kyra Panayia.
- 28-29 August, St John, at Vroukounda, Olympos (important feast at the cave of St John, beside the sea).
- 7 September, Panayia Larniotissa, near Pigadia.
- 8 September, Panayia Vrysiani, in Mesohori (one of the island's major festivals)
- 17 September, feast of Ayia Sofia, at Arkasa
- 3 November, feast of St George Methystis, at Othos, Pigadia, Spoa and other villages. This is the day celebrating the opening of the barrels containing the new wine. (People named George celebrate their name day on 3 November on Karpathos.)

*Regarding **cultural events**, the Municipality of Karpathos organises a number of concerts in the summer featuring traditional and modern music, as well as other events. Most of them take place in the courtyard of the Eparchio. In addition, a number of events take place in August, organised by «Omonia», the cultural association of Aperi.*

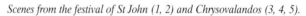

Scenes from the festival of St John (1, 2) and Chrysovalandos (3, 4, 5).

2

4

3

5

Musical tradition

Speaking of feasts and festivals, we should say a few words about how they are celebrated: i.e. with what music, songs and dances.

Regarding the music, there are three traditional **musical instruments** on Karpathos: the lyre, looks something like a violin, since it is also played with a bow; the lute which is somewhere between a guitar and a bouzouki and accompanies the lyre; and the tsambouna, a wind instrument that consists of a bag made of goat skin, fitted with a flute-like mouthpiece, the total somewhat resembles a bagpipe.

Traditional songs fall into three categories: folk songs (syrmatika), rhyming couplets (mantinades) and laments (mirologia). The syrmatika have an iambic metre (two syllables in a foot with the stress on the second) and a 15-syllable line; they include love songs, songs about the sea, about living far from home, etc. Their tunes are melodic, sweet and mainly slow, which is why they can be sung at a sit-down meal or at a sianos (= slow) or «lower» dance which we'll see later. Contrary to the syrmatika, the mantinades have a fast, lively beat. They consist of rhyming couplets and can be counted on to liven up every party. The Karpathians express themselves in mantinades at every joyous event, weddings, baptisms, feasts or festivals:

«When the son is baptised, let him live a thousand years
may he become a great tree with blossoms and branches
Good luck to the godfather, good luck to his parents
may all the years of his life always be happy.»

Mantinades are sung on other occasions as well. There is, for example, the patinada, a love song that is sung to the accompaniment of a guitar on the streets at night, and is strongly reminiscent of the nocturnal serenade (kantada) of the Ionian Islands.

«I sing in your district and don't take it too seriously,
a friend of mine loves you and I have the courage,
I pass by this street again where I am vowed not to
pass either alive or dead.»

1

1. Traditional dance at cultural event.
2. Musicians with their traditional musical instruments,
   lyre, lute and tsambouna, from the festival
   of St George at Vroukounda.

Dance

Music and singing accompany Karpathian dancing, which is present at all festivities. If the festival is being held in Olympos, then the visitor will have the unique pleasure of seeing women dancing in their traditional dress. The main dances are the sianos or «lower dance», which is accompanied by syrmatika songs, and the so-called pano horos («upper dance») which is fast and merry:

> «Listen to the lovely dance that people envy,
> Crete and Karpathos and Kassos dance it.
> In Crete they call it Cretan and in Kassos Sousta,
> in Karpathos pano horos, a delight to all tastes.»

There are also other dances in Karpathos, such as the zervos, (=left) because it is danced in the opposite direction from the others, the antipatitis, sousta and syrtis, which are all danced rarely and only in certain villages. The musicians –most of whom come from Menetes, the region which has the tradition of manufacturing the Karpathian lyre– usually stand in the middle of the square on a platform made of tables. Around them the dancers form a circle. The man at the head of the chain must be a good dancer because he plays a significant role here, and is followed by women.

Arts and letters

It is said that Karpathos is the island of university professors. There is much truth in this. Many of them are historians, involved with the folklore and sociology of their island. If one starts in the late 19th century, one finds first Emmanuel Manolakakis, whose book Karpathiaka, written in 1896, refers to the Dorian Resolution of Karpathos (translated from the French). This resolution, incised on a marble plaque found on the site of ancient Vrykous, provided valuable information about the history of the island. After Manolakakis came Michail G. Michailidis Niouaros, professor of literature, history and folklore, who has written a great deal about Karpathos and the Dodecanese more generally.

He was followed by contemporary scholars such as Kostis Minas, professor of the University of the Aegean, whose particular field consists of the linguistic idioms in Greece and particularly in Karpathos, and Minas Alexiadis, professor holding the Ethnography Chair at the University of Athens. Also worthy of note is the literary contribution of Georgios M. Georgiou, who wrote Karpathiaka, Vol I, that of Georgios A. Halkias, whose special interest is the folklore tradition of the village of Olympos, Vassos N. Vassilakis who, among other things, wrote Mesohori, Karpathos Vol. I, Konstantinos Melas, Manolis Makris, and others.

With respect to the arts and painting, there is Yannis Kapsis, a most productive folk artist and lyre-player who portrays scenes from the daily life of old-time as well as modern Karpathos in his works, which are usually small in size. We'll meet Yannis Kapsis again when we visit the village of Othos. There are also the painters Manos Anastasiadis in Diafani and Yannis Hatzivassilis in Olympos, who have shown their works in many one-man and group exhibitions, and Minas Vlachos, whose works have been presented in many exhibitions in Athens and other parts of the country.

The Karpathian house

In most villages, the traditional Karpathian house consists of the megalo spiti (large house), the official area used for feasts or as a bedroom, and the mikro (small), the kitchen or kello, as they call it in Olympos, with the fireplace used for cooking, in front of which the inhabitants of the island spend most of their day. If there is room, a paraspito (auxiliary house) is added and an oven, while a stone-paved courtyard with a small tree in the middle is considered virtually a necessity.

The root over the megalo spiti rests on a thick wooden beam called the mesa, which is supported by a wooden column (stylo) in the centre of the house. On the middle beam and the walls rest the cross-beams which are covered with seaweed. Special earth is pressed on top of the seaweed and becomes waterproof. Needless to say, the beam and the cross-beams have now become decorative, and the seaweed and earth have been replaced by concrete.

The outside door consists of two parts, upper and lower, and the windows are quite small. The spiti (house) is divided in two: a) the floor in front which is called patos and which is made of earth, or in the case of a mansion, is usually paved with white and black pebbles called cochladia, and b) the soufas, a wooden platform which is the main feature of the Karpathian house.

The soufas, where the entire family sleeps, is elevated; to get up there you ascend 2-3 steps in the middle of the room. This too is divided into two parts, the kato soufas and the panosoufi, which is one step higher.

The couple sleep on the kato soufas, while the panosoufi houses all the children. If there is a baby, it sleeps in a kounia (or hammock) that hangs above the children. Whatever is most precious to the family in terms of folk art hangs from the railing of the soufas: embroidered silk kerchiefs, lace, and colourful textile chramia or hangings, while the beds in the soufas are covered with blankets, quilts and cushions with

embroidered cushion covers. All around the walls are shelves adorned with three series of decorative plates. Particularly lavishly decorated with multicoloured textiles is the stylos, as pointed out earlier, which supports the middle beam of the roof and symbolises the pillar of the family. The space under the soufas is used for storage. Guests sit on the panga, a wide decorated couch situated vertically to the soufas, the inside of which is used to store cereals and other foods.

It is obvious from the above that every traditional Karpathian house is in itself a small folk museum.

Local materials such as stone and wood are mainly used on Karpathian houses. Karpathos always insists on tradition.

Pigadia.

4 PIGADIA

Beside the rocky hill that rises above the eastern coast of the island is Pigadia (or Karpathos town), the capital of the island and its main port. Pigadia (= wells), a name derived from the many wells in the region, is a relatively new town with about 1700 inhabitants. It has more than 20 hotels from second to fourth class, quite a few apartments with hotel facilities, and many rooms to rent.

Its houses, most of them new, do not conform to the traditional architecture that one tends to find in villages. Nevertheless the small, inner harbour with its multicoloured little boats moored around it, the town, the long sandy beach that comes afterward, and the green mountains with the stark white villages in the background create a delightful picture that ensures the visitor a good first impression.

(or Karpathos town)

It is believed that a Minoan citadel once stood on the rocky hill. We climb up a steep little street bypassing the paved road leading to Panayia Larniotissa. At the top of the hill are two carefully fenced private homes. To enjoy the view of the port and the town from this spot, we must ask permission from the owner who lives on the southwestern side. After crossing his property, we arrive at the edge of the cliff. Unfortunately only rocks remain, with no trace of ruins. It is explained that such traces may exist at a lower point, near the picturesque chapel that gazes out over the sea. But we can see not even a vestige of ruins at the top of the hill. The fact is however that in about 1000 BC, some thousand years after the Minoans, the Dorians arrived; and the largest of the four towns they established on the island was Potidaio or Poseidio, on the site of

The archaeological site at Potidaio.

present-day Pigadia. They must have used the previous citadel and even repaired it. It is also speculated that the sanctuary of Lindia Athena was built on the hilltop, as the sanctuary at Lindos was built on Rhodes. But this is a question that will engage archaeologists in the future, because to date no systematic excavations have taken place.

We may not have found ruins, but we were compensated by the wonderful view from this rock. At our feet is the port, the entire town of Karpathos, the gulf of Vronti with its endless beach and the mountain villages beyond. In the northwest is Aperi and Volada, with Othos and Menetes to the west.

We walk down from the acropolis to the port, Posi, as the locals call it, a word that is certainly derived from the ancient Poseidio. To our right, as we look at the sea, is the breakwater and the jetty at which the ferries are moored. In front of them is the port authority and an open space to serve the needs of the harbour. A small jetty offers moorage for boats and small craft. In front of the jetty the coast road is divided. One part of it is next to the sea, and relatively new, while the other, old road is higher up. They are linked by stairs situated at either end. Between them are little tables belonging to the sweet shops lined up along the road that are privileged with a superb view of the sea.

The church of Evangelistria.

LEGEND

1. Port Office

2. Taxi Rank

3. Buses Station

4. Tourist Offices

5. Bank

6. Church

7. Town Hall

8. Archaeological Museum

9. Post Office

10. Telecommunications

11. Police

12. Hospital

13. Informations

In about the middle of the harbour is the **church of Evangelistria**. It is at this point that the two roads go their separate ways with entire city blocks between them. The coastal road continues, full of restaurants, tavernas, bars and pizza parlours. And it is this road that during the summer has the most traffic. The view offered by the busy restaurants and tavernas with the candles lit on the tables is lovely. The great majority of the customers, and those strolling along the beach, are of course young people.

The coast road has reached a rocky shore on which is the Eparchio (or Regional Records Office) built by the Italians (see p. 19). It is a building with a small polygonal tower in the middle that dominates the region and stands out because of its architecture. Outside the **Eparchio**, in which various public services are housed, there is a space used as a children's playground and as an outdoor museum. Here one can see an early Christian marble baptismal font, architectural members that have been collected from various archaeological sites on the island, etc.

Past the Eparchio, the coastal road is deserted. There are no more coffee shops and tavernas as described above. Parallel to this coast road are two others that run through the inner part of the town. Most of the retail shops

44

in town are concentrated on these streets. In particular on the second one, 28th October St, are many public buildings such as the town hall, the post office and the police station. On the same street is the church of **Ayii Apostoli** (Holy Apostles), the main church in Pigadia, with a lovely carved icon screen. From the corner of Ayii Apostoli, the road sets out for the villages of Menetes and Arkassa, and for the airport as well; while the extension of 28th October St westward leads to **Vronti**, Pigadia's organised beach, and the mountain villages of Aperi, Volada, Othos and some others that we shall see later. The Pigadia beach extends over the whole length of the bay, more than 2.5 km. long. It has white sand and crystal clear waters. A little farther on is the Eparchio. On the first 1000 metres of the beach, umbrellas and deck chairs are available in the summer. Down the road a bit there are facilities for sea sports, especially wind surfing.

Areas near Pigadia

At a distance of some 1.5 km. from the town, beside the beach, are the ruins of the early Christian basilica of **Ayia Foteini**, which can be dated to the 5th or 6th century (see p. 15). Its marble columns and other architectural members are dramatically white against the deep blue of the sea. On the same site a Corinthian capital was found, as well as an inscription and a grave stele, all of marble. The church appears to have been built on the site of a former sanctuary of the Dioscuri.

There is a fair amount of interest in the coast east of Pigadia. It doesn't have a sandy beach, but rather a dense pine forest climbing up a steep hill. The paved road is fairly high up and offers a beautiful view of the sea. This is the road heading to the church of Panayia Larniotissa. It starts at the intersection with the little road up to the acropolis of ancient Potidaio.

The church of Ayii Apostoli (Holy Apostles)
and views of the harbour.

*Close by is the white chapel of **Ayios Petros**, seen against the background of the pine trees and the sea. Beyond, next to the road and on the edge of the cliff, a boulder with a hemispherical shape attracts our attention. A marble sign at its base informs us of the tradition surrounding this rock. Once, it says, a woman was bringing bread to the Virgin. At that point she tripped, and as she fell down she uttered profane oaths. At that very same moment, the bread she was carrying turned to stone and became the strange boulder.*

*We soon come to the church of **Panayia (Virgin Mary) Larniotissa** which is nestled among the pine trees on the top of the hill. It is a well cared for little church, freshly whitewashed, with its auxiliary areas and a large precinct that on 7 September hosts the visitors who come to pay their respects to the icon of the Virgin on her feastday and to take part in the great festivity that follows. On this same forested hill, but much higher up, is the church of Ayia Kyriaki, which is famous for its wonderful view of the surrounding*

area. But we can't get there from Panayia Larniotissa (because the road ends here), so we must find the alternate road that starts just after Pigadia, on the road to the airport. The church of **Ayia Kyriaki**, which stands dazzling white at the top of the hill, celebrates its feast day on 7 July, with the usual feasting etc.

The broader region of Pigadia used to be the centre of the island even in ancient times. Ancient Potidaio and its port were on a bay suitable for fishing and beside land that was appropriate for farming. This has been proved by the gravestones with the carved inscriptions that have been found dating mainly to the Classical and Hellenistic periods. There are other archaeological sites in the region as well, such as the Cave of Poseidon at the Mili site, on which a sanctuary has been discovered. This sanctuary may have been dedicated to the goddess Aphrodite, who was venerated in particular on the island. Arguing in favour of this version is the fact that statuettes of the goddess of love have been found in Pigadia.

Another interpretation, which cannot be ruled out, is that this sanctuary belonged to the Cave of the Virgin, which is about 2 kms. away. In the general area of Pigadia, both Minoan and Mycenean graves have been found.

1. The chapel of Ayios Petros.
2. The church of Panayia Larniotissa.
3. The beach east of Pigadia.
4. The organised beach of Vronti.
5. The church of Ayia Kyriaki.

4

5

SOUTHERN KARPATHOS

Amopi - Aphiartis
Makris Yialos
pp. 50 - 55

SOUTHWESTERN KARPATHOS

Menetes - Arkassa - Ayios Nikolaos
Paleokastro - Finiki
pp. 56 - 63

CENTRAL KARPATHOS

Aperi - Volada - Othos - Stes - Piles
Lefkos - Mesohori - Spoa
pp. 64 - 75

OLYMPOS & DIAFANI

Avlona - Vroukounda - Tristomo
(Northern Karpathos)
pp. 76 - 91

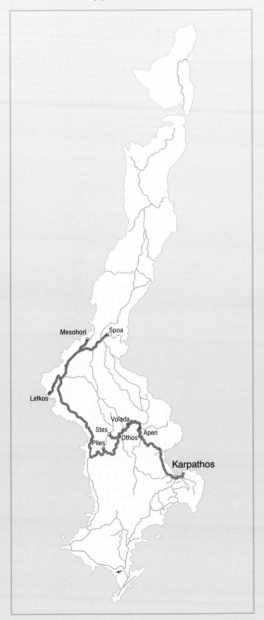

KARPATHOS

Amopi - Aphiartis
Makris Yialos

Amopi

It is almost impossible to believe what beauty can be found on in the beaches of Amopi unless you visit them. This also explains the rapid tourist development in the region.

To get from Pigadia to Amopi, we take the road heading southwest to the airport. Just outside the city we come to the intersection where the road to the left goes to Ayia Kyriaki, the church we spoke about in the previous chapter. The road rises steeply, soon offering a panoramic view of the town of Karpathos and its bay. After about 5 km, we can see the intersection leading to the village of Menetes, which can already be distinguished on the mountain to the right. In a while, we'll be leaving the main road and turning left toward the sea. The road narrows here and has many turns. Modern hotels and rooms to rent are dotted along the road, and in the distance we can see the tourist resort.

After 8.5 kms, we arrive in the centre of Amopi, where the bus terminal is located. Ahead of us, on a rocky outcrop into the sea, stands the lovely little church of **Ayii Apostoli**, which is visible from all sides, and celebrates its feast day on 29 June. We head toward it walking along the top of the rugged outerop. To our left we can see the main beach of Amopi among the pine trees. All along the horseshoe-shaped beach is white sand, which during the summer is scattered with colourful umbrellas and deck chairs and, of course, teaming with people. Around it there are some tavernas, bars and shops. Under the rocks, to the right, is a small jetty for mooring little vessels and boats.

To the right of this rocky outcrop is another beach, different from the first. It is straight, with fine pebbles and crystal waters. It is just a few metres wide because it is hemmed in by a five-metre cliff. It is perhaps this cliff that makes it so picturesque. Looking down on it from above, you can see its emerald waters glistening under the rays of the summer sun. Here too you'll find gaily coloured umbrellas and deck chairs, although fewer in number. Very close to the shore is a tiny rocky islet adding to the total visual effect. Strong swimmers often swim to and from it. This beach also has nearby tavernas and bars in a modern style, which lend a cosmopolitan atmosphere to the region. Another important fact is that all these beaches at Amopi are protected from the meltemia or summer winds.

These then are some of the reasons contributing to the significant development of Amopi in recent years. This is why more and

more people gather here in the summer:
to enjoy the lovely scenery in conjunction with
the tourist amenities. Moreover, the beaches
mentioned above may be the main beaches,
but they are by no means the only ones in the
area. Farther away, there are other graphic little
sandy coves such as Fokia and Lakki.

Amopi .

Aphiartis - Makris Yialos

We return to the main road and head toward the airport. On the way, we see the church of **Ayios Ioannis** painted white and blue. From here on, the landscape is mountainous and barren and the road, which has been climbing for a while, begins to descend. We soon see the panorama of **Aphiartis** and the bay of **Makris Yialos**. It is more than 5 km long. Its shore, which is rocky at the beginning, ends in a 2.5 km belt of sandy beach. Off the shore, in about mid-beach are two little islands, first Mira and then Prasonisi. The road now descends to some scrubby flats and follows a course parallel to the sand and about 500 m. away. Narrow gravel

roads lead down to the sea. There one can usually find a hotel, resting spot or facilities for wind surfing. These waters, together with the strong summer winds, are ideal for this particular sport. Some of these places have been given foreign names that have a certain allegorical significance. The first, with the strongest winds, is Devil's Bay. Its long-forgotten Greek name was Vatha and the ancient Greek name was Thaetho, taken from the significant city on the site. Farther along are Gun Bay and Chicken Bay, thus called because windsurfing lessons are given there to beginners and mainly to children. This is the southernmost point of Makris Yialos, a protected cove with shallow water that makes it look like a lake. Beside it is the chapel of Ayios Nikolaos and Ayia Anna, and beyond is the island's airport.

Near the airport, archaeological findings confirm that this region was inhabited as early as the 15th century BC, very likely by the Minoans. The eruption of the Santorini volcano in about 1500 BC affected not only Crete, but also, it would seem, part of Karpathos and in particular the southern part. On the eastern coast of nearby Crete, under about 35 metres of volcanic ash, archaeologists unearthed the fourth Minoan palace of Zakro. This ash appears to have covered the southern part of Karpathos as well, causing it to be deserted for many years. The promontory that protects the bay of Makris Yialos ends in a headland on which are the remains of the hull of a ship that was wrecked many years ago. Beyond is Kastello, another cape on the southernmost point of the island, whose name was derived from a medieval fortress built there by the Cornaro family, famous in the island's history. Nothing but some ruins remain of this fortress.

Behind the airport there is another sandy beach, **Elaris**, which may be even better than Makris Yialos. The airport is a total of 17 km. from Pigadia.

1. The Aphiartis beach.
2. The airport district.
3. The bay of Makris Yialos.
4. The church of Ayios Ioannis (St John).

Menetes

This white village looks like an eagle's nest perched high up on the slopes of the hill. We can see it from far away, as we approach from Pigadia, following the airport road. At the 5th km, we have to turn right and start ascending the barc mountain, proceeding on a paved road full of sharp turns. Fortunately, we reach the village, second largest on the island, after just 3 km. The road narrows, with houses and shops on either side, as it passes through the village. To the right, higher up, built on the edge of the cliff, is one of the most important churches on the island, the **Dormition of the Virgin**, *from which there is a wonderful view of the village and the surrounding hills. One is impressed by its roof, with its successive arches covered by red ceramic tiles, its high, tiered belfry and spacious courtyard. The church was built in the mid-19th century; inside we can see columns taken from the early Christian basilica of Ayia Anastasia near Paleokastro (See p. 59-60). The icon of the Virgin inside the church, which tradition tells us is miraculous, is much older. The church celebrates its feast day on 15 August with a great festival.*

Menetes: situated on a inaccessible hillside, this village was originally built to provide refuge from pirates for the island's inhabitants.

Arkassa - Ayios Nikolaos Paleokastro

The Arkassa region is an interesting one; it includes the picturesque village of the same name, an ancient acropolis (citadel) and a wonderful sandy beach. To get to the latter, we follow the road from Menetes heading toward the west coast of the island. A few kilometres down the road, the panorama of the Arkassa region opens out before us. The village of Arkassa is situated to the right. In the centre is a rocky peninsula on which are the ruins of the citadel of the ancient town. To our left is the lovely beach of **Ayios Nikolaos** and behind it the vast blue sea sparkling under the sun. We descend toward the sea. A road to the left leads us to the tourist settlement and ends in a

A festival is also held in the village on 6 August. To the left of the church of the Panayia there is a parking lot which represents an effort to solve the traffic problem in the village. From the church of the Dormition, we cross the village, heading up toward the hills, through narrow lanes, courtyards bedecked with flowers and, every so often, an attractive neoclassical building. Higher up, we reach a second, but much smaller parking area. The road leading here starts a long way outside the village. Over Menetes is the peak of the Profitis Ilias (Prophet Elijah, 509 m) with its chapel. Needless to say the view from here is the best of all. Other interesting churches in Menetes are those of Ayios Antonios, with its post-Byzantine wall paintings, and Ayios Mamas, which is outside the village on the way to Arkassa. The first buildings in Menetes were apparently built in the Middle Ages; today it has a population of 450. This village has a tradition in the construction of the Karpathian lyre, and most of the musicians on the island come from here.

1. The Dormition of the Virgin at the Menetes.
2. Paleokastro.
3. The chapel of Ayia Sofia (Divine Wisdom) and the mosaic from the early Christian church of Ayia Anastasia.

wonderful expanse of sand. The shallow water causes the waves to break many metres before the shore and create curved white lines. Swimming in this clear blue water is pure enjoyment, as is the sunset. At that time of day, the sun seems to be sinking between the two hills that protect the beach from the meltemia, the strong summer winds. The sandy area is fairly wide, and at the back of it are two rows of umbrellas and deckchairs, which don't take up much room. Behind the umbrellas, but a little higher up, is a refreshment stand serving as an additional amenity.

A rocky hill looms up over the right side of the beach. On it is **Paleokastro**, which we'll get to by the road that runs alongside the sea, north of Ayios Nikolaos. The road ends at the foot of the hill. At that point, to the left, is the church of **Ayia Sofia**, on the site of the former early Christian

basilica of Ayia Anastasia, which dates to the 4th-6th century. In front of the north wall of Ayia Sofia, a mosaic floor has been left uncovered and exposed to the wear and tear of time. This mosaic belonged to Ayia Anastasia, as did other valuable pieces that have now been preserved in the Rhodes Museum.

To get up to Paleokastro, we take the path leading upward at the end of the road. The ascent may be tiring, but you will be compensated both by the view and by what you will see there.

In fact, vestiges can be found there from all ages. Parts of the Cyclopean walls have been preserved from the Mycenean period, and there are traces from the period of Turkish rule as well. One theory has it that there may once have been a temple to Lindia Athena on this site.

Many of the archaeological findings from Paleokastro and the other regions of the island are kept in the little museum in Arkassa.

As we look around from the top of the hill, we can see most of the island. Right below our feet is the sandy beach of Ayios Nikolaos and the blue sea. Beyond is the cape of Ayios Theodoros and beside it the rocky islet of Diakoftis.

On the other side is the entire village of Arkassa and, a short distance away, the fishing village of Finiki.

We descend from Paleokastro and return to the main road that leads to Arkassa. For the past 2500 years, this village has borne, with a slight change, the name of the ancient town of Arkesia that once stood in the region.

Skylax, a geographer of the 4th century BC, and Strabo the historian who lived in the 1st century AD, both referred to the name of Arkesia as one of the four ancient towns on the island. We can also find the name of Arkesia on the lists of towns that paid tribute to Athens.

The village of Arkassa is built amphitheatrically over the sea, near Paleokastro. The gully through which the Ryaki creek flows divides it in two. The pretty church of the **Presentation of Christ (Ypapandi)** with its high bell-tower dominates one half. It celebrates its feast day on Candlemas, 2 February.

A bridge with a paved road crosses the gully, uniting the two parts of the village. Narrow roads, flower-bedecked courtyards, a good number of shops and a central square are some of the additional features of this picturesque village.

Arkassa, which has evolved into a tourist resort, has a lot of traffic in the summer, and is equipped to handle them with its hotels, apartments with hotel facilities and many rooms to rent. Arkassa has 400 permanent residents and is 16 km. from Pigadia.

1. The Archaeological Museum of Arkassa.
2, 3, 4, 5. Views of Arkassa.

Finiki

One and a half kilometres north of Arkassa and 17.5 km from Pigadia is the hamlet of Finiki. Its name is derived from the Phoenicians who used it as a trading post in the 11th century BC (see p. 16). Later the Dorians did likewise when Finiki was the harbour for ancient Arkesia. Many centuries later, it played a role of its own in the trade with Crete, neighbouring Kassos and the other islands in the Dodecanese.

It is worth looking around this picturesque fishing port. It has 80 permanent residents who are engaged mainly in fishing and tourism. In summer the village is full of tourists from other parts of Greece and abroad, because here people find what they are looking for: a small, clean and pretty beach near the hotel, pension or rented room they're staying in, several shops, modern bars and restaurants that serve fresh fish.

We turn left off the main road and head down toward the harbour. It is protected from the north wind by a rocky hill. Half way up the hill is the charming chapel of Ayios Nikolaos, which is snow white in colour but has a high blue domed roof and a smaller blue dome over the sanctuary. When we arrive at the harbour we see a fairly closed bay protected by rocks opposite the hill. Indeed, Finiki is a natural harbour. Alongside the road is the beach and beyond is a small concrete quay where colourful fishing caiques are moored. In the middle of the beach, a small bronze sculpture standing on a marble pedestal draws our attention.

The sculpture represents a little caique in which there are seven men. On the marble base

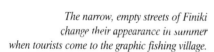

The narrow, empty streets of Finiki change their appearance in summer when tourists come to the graphic fishing village.

of the monument we read the inscription:

THIS BOAT OF SALVATION «IMMAKOLATA»
IS DEDICATED TO THE HEROIC
MICHAIL PITTAS
KONSTANTINOS LAMBRIDIS
EMMANUEL PATSOURAKIS
LAZAROS KOSMAS
SOPHOCLES ECONOMIDIS
NIKOLAOS STAMATAKIS
GEORGIOS CHRISTODOULOS
WHO ON 8-10-1944 SET OUT FROM FINIKI IN THE «IMMAKOLATA»
FOR ALEXANDRIA, BEARING THE MESSAGE
TO THE GREEK GOVERNMENT [in exile]
OF KARPATHOS'S REVOLT [against the Nazi occupation].

The inscription says it all. The only thing we can add here is that it took the little caique five days to reach Egypt.

The mountain villages of gleaming white, high on Mount Lastos that rises to almost 1000 metres, belong to central Karpathos. They were built at altitudes of between 300 and 500 metres and draw the attention of visitors, who can see them from Pigadia, as they drink their coffee in the harbour coffee shops, or enjoy the

KARPATHOS

es - Lefkos - Mesohori - Spoa

summer sun on a beach. One day they should go up to explore them and from there descend to the west coast, a lovely itinerary. The road to these villages is paved and in very good condition; it heads northwest initially, parallel to the beach, follows it for a long way and then starts to ascend in sharp turns.

Aperi - Volada

The first village we meet, 8 km out of Pigadia, is **Aperi**. Once capital of the island, it continues to this day to be the episcopal see of the Metropolitan of Karpathos. It was built in the Middle Ages when the inhabitants of Pigadia withdrew to the interior of the island in fear of repeated pirates' raids. In fact, Aperi, which is in a small ravine, cannot be seen from the sea. Our first view of it is magnificent. The road crosses a verdant ravine and cuts the village in two. It has pretty, well-kept houses, with little gardens, trees, and flowers. But it is also an aristocratic village, boasting a few villas built by Greeks from America who come back to the island every year for their holidays. A wealthy village; one of the wealthiest in Greece, it is said.

We pause for a moment on the right side of the road to enjoy the view. Below, in the ravine, a bridge joins the two slopes. Opposite is a large church roofed with ceramic tiles. It is the **Panayia**, the island's cathedral, and beside it is a large building which houses the diocesan offices and the residence of the bishop. There is a hill over the village, on top of which is the acropolis of ancient Karpathos. The village appears to have been built in the Middle Ages, but the region around it had been inhabited much earlier. This is shown by the findings from Lastos, which were dated to the Early Bronze age, the Minoan period and later. There, too, on the acropolis of ancient Karpathos, a castle was built that was used by Venetians and Turks alike.

Aperi, at an altitude of 320 m., has 400 permanent residents and still occupies a special place in the island's social and cultural life. This is one of the reasons why it has many visitors, especially in summer. Moreover, it is the starting point or at least a way station «on land» to what are perhaps the most picturesque beaches on Karpathos, **Ahata** (5km) and **Kyra-Panayia** (7km) which we'll be seeing in another chapter. It is also the starting point for travelling to other interesting places that are not on the coast, such as the church of Ayios Georgios in Vatses and the tiny green settlements of **Katodi** (4 km) and **Mertona** (4 km) which are near Kyra-Panayia.

After Aperi the road keeps ascending and two km later, brings us to the village of **Volada**. This village is at 440 m. and offers a wonderful view of Pigadia and the southern section of the island. Its white houses are highlighted against the rocky mountain slope, and its narrow cobbled streets and old houses have the feeling of a Cycladic village. The only exceptions to the white are

the red tiles on most roofs. The most important church in the village is the 18th-century Panayia, which celebrates its feast day on 8 September. Below the village there is a lot of greenery, mainly from fruit trees, while some 100 m. above it is a small but dense forest and then the bare rock of the mountain.

1. The Cathedral of Karpathos in the village of Aperi.
2. The village of Volada.
3. Othos, the highest village on Karpathos.

Othos - Stes

Othos is the highest village on Karpathos (510 m.) and one of the most interesting. It is a pleasure to taste the local specialties, especially the famous Karpathian sausages, while sitting in one of the two tavernas located on the main road. It is splendid to look out over the panorama of the eastern coast of the island fading away in the vastness of the sea. We cross the village and find the **Folklore Museum** on the main street. Yannis Kapsis, the man whose purpose in life is to maintain the island's traditions, has the key.

2

3

His talents are many; he plays the lyre, the Karpathian lyre, and teaches young people to play it as well. Often he accompanies himself on the lyre as he sings. But his main occupation seems to be painting. He paints pictures, large and small, from the life of Karpathos. We found him in his studio, which is on the main street, just beyond the Museum. The studio is small, but the walls are all hung with his works. And looking at them one can't help but call to mind Theophilos, the folk artist from Mytilene. The artist accompanied us from his studio to the Folklore Museum, which includes a replica of the interior of a traditional Karpathian home.

Still on the main street, and just before leaving the village, to the right, is the pretty church of the **Dormition of the Virgin**, with a fountain in its courtyard. Othos is famous for the many festivals, almost ten, held in it. The main ones are the feasts of Ayios Panteleimon on 26-29 July, Ayios Georgios Methystis on 3 November, the last day before Lent (Apokria), and Clean Monday, the first day of Lent.

From Othos, which has 230 permanent inhabitants and is 12 km from Pigadia, we head now toward Piles. One km later, a road to the right soon leads us to **Stes**. This is a quiet little village built on the Lastos plateau, and looks like a forgotten paradise. All around it is greenery, mainly vineyards. They say that the best wine on the island comes from here. There is also the

Church of the Dormition of the Virgin in Othos.

attractive church of Ayios Panteleimon which celebrates its feast day between 26-28 July. North of Stes is the little settlement of Lastos with its few farmhouses. A mountain road leads to it, and another, alongside which is the cliff, cuts through the rock of the mountain and stops at the point where the path starts up to the top of Mount **Kali Limni**, the highest mountain on Karpathos (1215 m). The landscape is untamed, imposing, and the view towards the sea and the western coast of the island is spectacular.

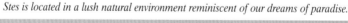

Stes is located in a lush natural environment reminiscent of our dreams of paradise.

Piles - Lefkos

After our visit to Stes, we return to the main road and head for Piles. To our left, on a green hill is the church of Ayios Georgios (St George). The road descends in sharp turns from 500 to 300 m. Soon we can see the first houses of **Piles**. We leave the main road leading to the sea and turn right. We enter the village, following a narrow road that crosses it from one side to the other. From the road we can see its two-storey houses with colourful doors, windows, verandas or balconies full of bouganvillaea, and its narrow lanes with courtyards from which bougainvillaea and other ornamental plants.

The village is built on the side of the mountain, which is why most of the houses look out over the sea. Piles has 235 permanent residents which in summer become many more. It is 15 km from Pigadia.

The old road from Piles to Lefkos is a shorter route and passes through a pine forest. But it's a gravel road and not in very good condition, which is why people usually travel to Lefkos by the main road which goes down to the sea from Othos and then takes the coast road. So we too will follow the paved road. Three kilometres later, after a continuous descent, we reach the coast road. The turn to the left goes to Finiki, Arkassa, and Menetes. We take the right turn to Mesohori. In a little while we are driving along one of the most beautiful parts of the route. We are under Kali Limni, the highest mountain on the island, with its steep slopes, scored by verdant ravines of pine trees that reach down as far as the deep blue of the sea. Alongside the road is a spring whose water must come from much higher up. Below, on the coast, a sandy beach beckons,

offering us an unforgettable swim. The beach is called **Adia** and has a few rented rooms, a small campground and one restaurant.

After this lovely coastal landscape, the road ascends again in a series of sharp turns. We drive through a pine forest and then gaze out on the sea again. To the northwest, we can see a headland and next to it an islet. In front of the islet, like white brushstrokes, some beaches and a tiny settlement can be discerned. It is the famous hamlet of Lefkos (=white). It looks serene. The terrain is almost flat. The mountain, with its lush gullies, is quite far away to the right. We descend and at the intersection, we leave the paved road and turn left. Approaching the sea, we reach another crossroads. The road to the left leads to the first of the many beaches in the region. It is **Akroyiali** or **Potali**, a secluded beach with very few bathers. We continue on to the right, driving in the direction of **Lefkos**. A surprise awaits us: we find ourselves on a picturesque, horseshoe-shaped cove with dazzling white sand. This beach has organised facilities. The sea is calm and shallow, and is not ruffled by any wind. It is 32 km. from Pigadia. On the side of the cove opposite the beach, there are a few houses, coffee shops and tavernas and a quay full of little fishing caiques whose bright colours are reflected in the calm waters of the sea. We head down to Limani (=port) as everyone calls the cove.

1. Lane in Piles.
2. The Adia beach.
3. Akroyiali: an ideal beach for anyone who wants to avoid the crowds.
4. Limani is what everybody calls the cove at Lefkos.

3

4

Yellow fishermen's nets are spread out on the quay. Somewhere close by there are also traces of an early Christian basilica from the 5th century. We walk past the houses, and another cove appears before us. Lefkos is full of coves, most of which are sandy. This second cove is protected by a little peninsula and a rocky islet. Everywhere you look in Lefkos is a scene to be enjoyed. So we walk out onto the little peninsula. It is low but rocky. Behind it is a third cove, this time larger and more open, which is protected from the summer winds by the little island of Sokastro.

Here is an organised sandy beach called **Frankolimnionas**. At its north edge, a large hotel has been built. A second, smaller hotel is situated at the entrance to the settlement, and there are many rooms to rent in the little port we saw earlier. As we can see, there has been major tourist development in the region owing to its natural beauty.

But natural beauty isn't the only reason for the development of Lefkos. It is also of major archaeological interest. On the islet of **Sokastro** mentioned above, for example, ruins from the Byzantine and medieval periods can be found. Tradition tells us that it was the launching point of Nicephorus Phocas's campaign to liberate Crete from the Arabs in the 10th century AD.

On the Rizes site, ruins of houses have been unearthed and, some distance from the coast, is the Byzantine church of **Ayios Georgios**, built in the 13th century, and decorated with wall paintings that have been greatly damaged by time.

1. The church of Ayios Georgios in Lefkos.
2. The organised beach at Frankolimionas.
3. The beach at Lefkos.
4. Mesohori.

Mesochori - Spoa

Leaving the lovely hamlet of Lefkos, we return to the main road from Piles or Arkassa. At the crossroads, we take the left turn toward Neohori. We have once again entered the pine forest and are following a route which is one of the loveliest on Karpathos. At the beginning, the road rises steeply. But in a little while we come to the crossroads with the road that leads to Spoa and we turn left.

Driving around one turn, we can just make out an unforgettable view among the pine trees. Far in the distance is the town of **Mesohori**,

4

admire the snow-white houses with their courtyards full of flowers.

Many of these houses are traditional, and have the outdoor areas paved with pebble mosaics. On the interior, wood is the decorative element that dominates. As we proceed, we come to a square at the edge of the village. We are now 150 m. above the sea looking out over a unique sunset. In this square are located two of the many churches in Mesohori. One is Stavros (= Cross) and the other is Ayios Nikolaos; both were built in the 18th century. But the most important church in the village and perhaps on the entire island is Panayia Vrysiani, which was so named because it is built over the only spring (= vrysi) in Mesohori. The exterior of the church is imposing, with its high bell-tower built in about 1935, as is its interior. On the same site was once a smaller church built in about 1553 which was too small to hold all the worshippers, and that was why it had to be enlarged. Its feastday is celebrated on 8 September, when people gather here, not only from Karpathos, but from neighboring Kassos as well, to attend the most splendid festival on the island, with food and an all-night party with local dances and songs.

Another noteworthy church in the village is that of Aï Yiannis Prodromos (St John the Baptist). Its remarkable wall paintings have contributed to its being declared an archaeological site. There are a further five churches in Mesohori and many chapels (xoklesia) scattered around the countryside from the Lefkos cove (see above, Lefkos, church of Ayios Georgios) to the Ayia Irini cove. We can go to the Ayia Irini cove on foot over a rough and hazardous goat track, or better still in a little caique from Kafkalo, the hamlet below Mesohori. This is a lovely beach with pebbles and sand under a vertical rock. Of the old church of Ayia Irini, only its sanctuary has been preserved, which is half-buried under the sand. Its festival is on 5 May. Mesohori (= Middle Village) is in approximately the middle

perched high over the sea. Next to it are two coves separated by a small headland, and behind them, as though carved out by a knife, is an enormous rock which protects them from the north wind. The top of the rock is a curved line. It is the continuation of the Kymara range, «suspended» over the sea. We approach it. We cross a bridge over a gaping chasm. From here we can see Mesohori better: white houses, jostling each other closely, most of them with flat roofs. A few of them have red tile roofs. Around the village there is a great deal of green space and right behind them the mountain looms majestically. The sea, dark blue in the open sea and choppy in the wind, becomes azure blue and calm farther inland toward the two coves, especially the second, Ayia Irini, which is tucked in a corner.

We can't enter the village by car, so we leave it in a parking area past Mesohori that has been created by the widening of the road. This is an opportunity to walk through the narrow streets, to climb up and down their stone steps, and to of the island, hence its name, and is 34 km from Pigadia, via Piles (on the new coast road). Isolated owing to the poor condition of the road up to just a few years ago, Mesohori has kept up its customs and manners, many of which are similar to those of Olympos, about which more will be said later. Its 350 permanent residents are chiefly engaged in farming and less so with sheep and goat-herding. The village is surrounded by olive groves and vineyards and produces large quantities of olive oil and wine. Karpathos is famous in particular for the quality of its wine.

1. Stepped laneway in Mesohori.
2, 3. Abandoned windmills in the village of Spoa and view of the same village.

From Mesohori we return to the crossroads of the road to **Spoa** and turn left. This is the narrowest point on the island, and after a short drive through the pine forest, we can see the east coast. We realise the village is nearby when we see its abandoned mills standing in a row. Soon we can see Spoa. Built on the mountain slope at an altitude of 350 m., its residents have a lovely view of the sea. It is preceded by a district on a low hill. Then there's a street with two or three coffee shops on it, where you can have a snack.

A deep green gully is next and then the main part of the village, which slopes gently down into a little green valley.

Spoa is a fairly small village with about 200 inhabitants, and is 24 km from Pigadia on the gravel road that passes through Aperi at the 16-km point, and 38 km from Piles on the paved road we have followed so far.

The port serving Spoa is the little hamlet of **Ayios Nikolaos**, which you reach over a poor road about 5 km long.

8 OLYMPOS

We are now in the northern part of the island, isolated and wild. It is isolated because the 45-km road that links it with the capital Pigadia is not in very good condition and wild because its mountains are steep rock. There is forest only between Olympos and Diafani. In this region, there are sites which, when you see them, you feel awe and admiration at the same time. One of them is Olympos, the village with a history going back 1200 years. Fortunately for this village, it has an outlet to the sea, since its port Diafani is linked to it by a 9-km paved road.

The valleys are few and small. The largest and most important of them is that of Avlona, north of Olympos, where the rural settlement of the same name is located.

& DIAFANI

Avlona - Vroukounda - Tristomo

On the northwestern tip of Karpathos was the ancient town of Vrykous, in the vicinity of which the little chapel of Aï-Yianni (St John) is tucked into a cave. And finally at the northern end of the island there is the protected bay of Tristomo, a worthwhile region owing to both its geographical location and its historical background, since it was the port of the ancient town of Vrykous, and served as a harbour in later years as well, up to the Revolution of 1821.

Olympos

This village, famous for its tradition and folklore, was first built between the 7th and 9th centuries when the inhabitants of Vroukounda, who suffered from the successive pirate raids, were obliged to abandon the coast and seek safety in the mountains of the remote hinterlands. They selected one of the most inaccessible regions, which was located between the grey-black mountain massifs of Aï-Ilias (718 m.) and Koryfi (588 m.). And for even greater protection, they built a castle that embodied their houses. The few ruins that can still be seen today, and the names of the districts Mesa Kastro and Oxo Kamara in the village, testify to the presence of this castle. This was during the early centuries of its habitation. Later, when the village grew and there was no longer room for the houses within the wall, they began being built outside it. This expansion notwithstanding, the isolation from the rest of the world continued. And the result of it was that virtually nothing changed with the passage of time. The traditional architecture of their homes remained unaltered. The same was true of the interior layout and decoration. Given these facts, the entire village is today a museum. But tradition was not observed only with respect to the buildings. The customs and manners, songs, and behaviour of its inhabitants remained the same. Even their language sustained minimal changes. This is why their speech still contains elements from the Doric dialect which are very rarely heard in Greece.

We spoke earlier of the fact that the village was isolated until recently. That's because people have «discovered» it and an increasing number of visitors are now going to Olympos. Its inhabitants were surprised at the beginning. But then they understood. They understood that their village must have something very special in order to attract so

many visitors. So they shouldn't change anything. Women should continue to wear their colourful traditional dress. And indeed, you go there, you see them and you are amazed. And you hesitantly ask permission to photograph them. They agree, simply, proudly, and before you even have time to adjust your camera lens, they have already taken a pose with their head high and a restrained but confident smile on their lips.

These are the people of Olympos. But it is time to take a walk and see its sights. Cars driving up from Diafani or coming straight from Pigadia must park in a widening of the road just before the entrance to the village, where you will also find the first restaurants. Then we enter the village, following the main street that runs through it from east to west. To our left, houses climb up the side of a steep, bare mountain, that of **Ayios Ilias**, whose name was derived from the chapel of the Prophet Elijah on its peak. This magnificent, cone-shaped mountain was apparently named Olympos in ancient times. And it was from here that the village took its name. On the right-hand side of the street is a row of traditional little tavernas each of which has a narrow veranda at the back overlooking the deep gorge. The specialty of these tavernas is makarounes, a kind of homemade pasta. Most of the shops are situated on the same street. They display the local folk-art products on their walls for visitors to see, mainly textiles, dresses, ceramics, etc.

We walk up a steep street and finally arrive at Platy, a tiny little square in which festivals take place, weather permitting. A small wooden platform is set up in the middle of the square, on which the musicians take their places. Women in traditional dress dance in circles around it.

Beside Platy is the village's main church, the 16th-century **Dormition of the Virgin** with a carved gilt wooden icon-screen and some wonderful wall-paintings, which constitute characteristic examples of Byzantine art. It celebrates its feastday on 15 August, with one of the more significant festivals in the village. Another noteworthy but smaller church in Olympos is that of Ayios Onufrios, built in the 12th century.

1. The main coffee shop in Platy.
2, 3. The sale of folk art products has contributed
   to the island's tourist develoment.
4. The church of the Dormition of the Virgin.

4

East of the church of the Dormition, clinging to the top of the Ayios Ilias slope, are the famous windmills, built in the shape of a horse-shoe, abandoned and dilapidated, reminding us of times past.

We leave Platy and descend westwards. Soon we are enjoying a superb view. We are 150 m. above the sea, the Aegean is spread out in front of us in all its glory; the waves are crashing against the rocky coast leaving a white brushstroke in their wake. Beside us we can see most of the village hugging the hillside and far beyond we can make out the highest mountains of Karpathos. One of them is Kymaras, with its characteristic «hump» hanging over the sea. Behind it is Mesohori, which we visited in a previous chapter.

We keep going downhill, following the spiralling road that leads us to the ridge between Ayios Ilias and Koryfi. The view we have in front of us is perhaps the most magnificent and most characteristic of the village. Because on top of the ridge are another four windmills, two of which are turning, with their white sails billowing in the air, grinding wheat as they have been doing for centuries. These windmills, with the black mountain Koryfi in the background, are a source of inspiration for artists and photographers who come to immortalise this wonderful sight. A walk through the village should end with a visit to a traditional house (see p. 34). We won't find any major differences between it and traditional houses in other villages. In Olympos, space may be a little more cramped, but here too there is the megalo spiti (literally, «large house») which is by itself, and alongside it is the auxiliary area, the kitchen and its fireplace which is called the kello. Here, too, the megalo spiti is divided into the patos, the lower part of the room, and the soufas, the elevated wooden platform, and the even higher structure called the panosoufi; the walls all around are adorned with shelves displaying colorful plates and mugs. It is said that the decoration of the soufas with the local

As long as the wind can still move the sails on the windmills, Olympos will remain nostalgically attached to the customs of bygone ages.

textiles and embroideries is more striking here in Olympos than in the other villages, as is the traditional women's dress. The truth is that only in Olympos has this dress been retained: the everyday dress, with its plain-coloured embroidered apron and simple head kerchief worn by many elderly and middle-aged women, and the other, official, colourful dress worn by all women at the village festivals, with two rows of gold coins covering almost their entire chest. (See p. 27)

It is worth noting that Olympos has some of the largest festivals on the island (see p. 30).

There are about 300 permanent residents in Olympos now, although just after the war there were as many as 1500. Their main occupations were as farmers and livestock-breeders.

Their efforts were devoted to making every bit of this barren, rock-strewn land arable, leaving not a centimetre unexploited. It was gruelling work and life was harsh, which was why people started migrating. People moved to Athens and to other places in Greece, but mainly they went to the United States. Many of them today live in Boston; they come back at least every two years to spend their vacations in the village. And their girls, who speak broken Greek, proudly wear their colourful traditional dress at the festival, imitating their mothers or grandmothers and thus carrying on the tradition. Those who stayed behind in Olympos are now trying out new occupations in tourism. They have remodelled their houses to offer rooms for rent; they have rented shops in which to sell folk art items, and tavernas to serve the visitors whose numbers are increasing every year. The ranks of the farmers and shepherds have dwindled dramatically, as have others who were mainly employed in traditional crafts. A characteristic example is the fact that there is just one shoemaker left who makes the traditional stivania (a type of boot).

Olympos: where time has stood still.

Avlona - Vroukounda - Tristomo

A gravel road that begins about half way along the road from Diafani to Olympos heads north and takes us to **Avlona**. It is a long, narrow valley that opens out onto the northern coast of the island, with the settlement of the same name built amph-theatrically on the slopes of the mountain to the east. Its earth is brown in colour and the terrain flat, separated by drystone fences into individual properties; it used to be the bread-basket of Olympos. The road crosses the valley and arrives at the settlement, consisting of about 300 cottages or «stables» as the local people call them. Most of these cottages have today been abandoned. In the past they were used as summer cottages, since almost all the inhabitants of Olympos and Diafani had to live in Avlona in summer to do their farm chores, such as reaping, threshing, storing cereals and hay, etc.

From Avlona, after an hour's drive north, we come to a very interesting region. The ruins of **Vrykous**, one of the four ancient towns of Karpathos, can be seen near the sea. From these finds, among which are rock-hewn tombs, it is obvious that the region had been inhabited as early as the

Minoan or Mycenean periods, although the name must have been given to it by the Dorians. The period of its greatest prosperity was in the 4th and 3rd centuries BC. This is shown by the part of the ancient town's wall which has been preserved and which belongs to the Hellenistic age.

In any event, Vrykous continued to be inhabited up to the Christian period. But in about the 8th century, its inhabitants, terrified by the successive raids by Arabs and by pirates in general, were obliged to desert the village and flee to the mountains. In another version of the migration, a terrible earthquake devastated the region and destroyed the town, causing the mass exodus. The possibility that the emigration was caused by both events cannot be ruled out.

Near the ruins, and specifically on the rocky headland of a small peninsula, the well-known chapel of Ayios Yiannis (St John) was found inside a cave. It celebrates its feastday on 29 August with all the ceremony dictated by tradition. Most of the inhabitants of Olympos and Diafani arrive there on 28 August. Women wear their official traditional dress and the feasting continues all night long. Of course the mood is devout during the service held in the cave of St John, which is lighted with candles and torches, since there is no electricity in the area, which is known today as Vroukounda or Vourgounda.

Northeast of Vroukounda, just below the northernmost tip of Karpathos, is **Tristomo**, the lovely natural harbour of ancient Vrykous. At its entrance there are two rocky islets that create three mouths, which explains its name (Tristomo= three mouths). This harbour, since it is absolutely safe and the only one in the broader area, has played a significant role in both ancient and modern times. In Tristomo there are some cottages but there is some question as to whether even one shepherd lives there.

North of Tristomo is the **Steno** (=Strait), a channel just 200 m. that separates Karpathos from the island of Saria, which we shall see later. In this region and especially on the site of the chapel of Ayia Ekaterini (St Catherine), there is speculation that a temple of Porthmios Poseidon, who was worshipped throughout Karpathos, may have stood.

1, 2, 3. Scenes from the festival of St John in Vroukounda.
4. Aerial view of Tristomo.

4

Diafani

The picturesque port that serves Olympos is at the same time the second-largest harbour on the island. The ferries that sail two or three times a week from Pigadia dock at Diafani. But apart from the ferries, there are small boats that sail every day from Pigadia to Diafani and back. During the summer, these boats are full because they are carrying visitors who will later take the bus to go up to Olympos.

As you approach Diafani from the sea, the first impression is of a pretty village. Laid out around a little pebbled bay, it is surrounded by low hills covered by pine trees behind which are the high mountains of Olympos. In the middle of the inlet, the jetty at which the boats tie up is a fish wharf with its multicoloured caiques; lined up opposite are restaurants, coffee shops and tavernas. On the hill with the pine trees, to the left, two or three dilapidated windmills remind one of the old times, when they were constantly in motion grinding wheat. Standing among the two-storey houses are three churches whose domes are covered with red tiles. The largest of these is the Zoodohos Piyi (Fount of Life).

Diafani appears to have been inhabited since the Minoan period, as testified by the vestiges of the ruins found in the Kambi gulf, south of the port. But wherever this settlement was, even if it had been preserved up to the period of the pirates' raids, it could only have had the same fate as the other coastal settlements such as Pigadia and Vroukounda. That is, it was abandoned by its inhabitants, who sought a safer place to live in the remote mountains of Olympos. But at some point, these raids stopped and the self-exiled people gradually returned from the mountains, seeking an outlet onto the sea. It is said that the beginning took place early, but the Diafani we see today was built by the residents of Olympos in the mid-19th century. From then on the town began to grow rapidly. There was never a road to Olympos from Pigadia in the past, and even today, when such a road exists, the village is supplied from Diafani. Thus a small tourist resort was created with a few

hotels and a number of rooms to rent in which visitors are offered the warm hospitality of the local people which constitutes a guarantee of pleasant holidays. Moreover Diafani can be used as a base for many interesting excursions, such as to the island of Saria which we'll be visiting next, or to the beaches to which two small vessels go. If Diafani itself is not sufficient for one's daily swim, the lovely beach of **Vananda** with its pebbles, pine trees and oleanders is just 20 min. away on foot.

1, 2, 3. Views of Diafani.
4. Vananda beach.

9

THE EASTERN COAST

From Pigadia to Diafani

The most delightful beaches on the island's eastern coast can be found in this region. High mountains with rocky slopes descend sharply into the sea, forming coves, large and small, edged with dazzling white sand. Just a few years ago, this was also the site of Karpathos's most beautiful pine forest. But a huge forest fire that burned for days out of control devastated most of it. Thus it happens that the western coast, which remained untouched by fire, today has more greenery. Despite this loss, the eastern coast of the island continues to be the more picturesque. The crystal waters of the sea, with their amazing colours and precipitous rocks embracing sandy beaches have lost nothing of their earlier beauty. In any event, not all the pine trees were burned. A good many have been saved in gullies and new seedlings are now starting gradually to sprout, which will one day make the mountain slopes green again.

Every day during the summer caiques set out from Pigadia on regular day trips heading for these beaches. People hasten to take advantage of this opportunity to get to know these beaches and to enjoy a swim in their clear waters. Of course it isn't possible to see them all in one day! You can visit one, two or at most three, and these

will be the nearest ones. You will have an opportunity to visit the more distant ones from Diafani, which is closer to them. We will look at them all, taking them in order, one by one.

Driving around the steep promontory of Pigadia bay, we'll go first to **Ahata**, the magical little cove surrounded by enormous rocks descending almost vertically into the sea. The Profitis Ilias hill (499 m.) is on one side and Anginara (600 m.) on the other.

It is perhaps the smallest beach with the most unspoiled beauty. Northwest of Ahata is the most picturesque beach on Karpathos, **Kyra-Panayia**. As on Ahata, there are vertical rocks plunging into the sea, but the bay is bigger, the beach is wider, the pine trees are suspended over the sea, and the white church of Kyra-Panayia with its red tiled dome, high up on the edge of the bay, gives its own characteristic tone to the landscape. This church was apparently built in 1833 by a ship's captain in thanksgiving for his survival when his ship ran aground in this cove in a storm. It is also known that during the War of Independence in 1821, a dockyard operated here for the needs of the Revolution. During recent years, the beach has been organised. It has umbrellas to provide shade from the sun and deck chairs;

inland a small tourist resort has been created with rooms to rent and restaurants. Above Kyra-Panayia are the verdant sites of Katodi and Mertonas.

Fairly close to Kyra-Panayia is a new, larger and, one might say, more idyllic beach, **Apella**. Here, behind the white sand there are pine trees that offer their shade to bathers. The colour of the sea, emerald green near the sand, becomes deep blue as the water gets deeper. Near the shore, the neglected Byzantine chapel of Ayios Loukas (St Luke), inside a rock, is of interest. This is a 12th-century church, among whose damaged wall paintings is a significant one of St John the Baptist.

Beauty in four scenes:
Kapi (1), Ahata (2), Opsi (3), Apella (4).

The gravel road that goes from Aperi to Spoa and Olympos runs high up over the beach. Continuing our trip northward, we arrive at **Ayios Nikolaos** (St Nicholas), the graphic little harbour and port of the village of Spoa (see Central Karpathos), with which it is linked by a very steep gravel road 5 km long. Some of the residents of Spoa, even though they are farmers and stockbreeders, have a small fishing caique or even just a rowboat to fish with. So it isn't at all strange to be eating fish, the delicious parrot fish that are plentiful in these waters, not only in Ayios Nikolaos but even in Spoa which is at an altitude of 350 m. From Ayios Nikolaos and beyond, we are sailing alongside the steep, rocky shores neighbouring on Olympos and Diafani. To our left, is the beach of **Agnontia** and then that of **Ayios Minas**, which is well known for its lovely sand. Another of its features is the high hill to the right, which protects it from the summer winds. At the top of the hill can be seen the stark white chapel of Ayios Minas, from which the beach took its name.

After Ayios Minas, we enter the open bay of **Nati** with its blue-green water and smooth pebbles. The beach is one of the favourites of swimmers from Diafani who are attracted by its spaciousness and crystal waters. A little farther north is the smaller beach of **Kapi**, suitable for swimmers who like to get away from the crowds, and beyond that the better known **Forokli** with its fine sand. Next to Forokli is **Opsi**, another beach reminiscent of Kapi, which we visited a little earlier, except that this one is even smaller. We sail around the Makria Pounda headland and approach the last beach before Diafani, **Papa-Minas** which is surrounded by rocks. All these beaches up as far as Ayios Minas are easy to get to in summer from Diafani, from which little excursion caiques set out every day.

Unique Karpathos beaches:
1. Ayios Minas.
2. Papa-Minas.,
3. Ayios Nikolaos.
4. Nati.

4

We have left Diafani and are sailing north with Saria as our destination. As we pass through the strait just 200 m. wide that separates the two islands and sail alongside the rocky coasts of Saria, not one of us could have imagined that this trip would have included such a surprise. But there we were, sailing toward **Palatia**, Saria's harbour. The name alone (which means palaces) conceals something from myth or history that should have prepared us.

For the time being, we find that the sheer rock to our left is very high for such a small island. It says on the map that it is 630 m. high. The boat sails close to the shore. The water is deep and dark blue in colour. As we approach the little harbour the rocks loom even more magnificently. Just beyond it, a high rock rises out of the sea and then another, smaller one, as though they were natural beacons to warn ships' captains approaching the island. The water here is azure in colour and sparkling under the sunlight. In a while we enter the closed bay, where the real surprise starts. To the right and left are rocks that give the impression of forming a high dock. The colour of the sea is blue-green, and on the inlet of the bay is a beach with little white pebbles surrounded by tamarisk trees offering their shade to visitors. Most visitors can't resist this unexpected temptation and dive right into the sea.

For them, this is a paradise on earth, and they certainly have a point. But we must press on in order to see as much as possible.

e surprise came at the end

First of all, on these rocks which, as noted earlier, resemble a high dock, hollows have been carved out indicating that an ancient port once existed there. This port may possibly have served the town of Nisyros, one of the four Dorian towns on Karpathos (Tetrapolis). This account is based on artifacts found in the region, among which were architectural members from early Christian churches and other buildings that came later. But the region may have been inhabited much earlier than the building of Nisyros, perhaps even as early as the Neolithic age. This possibility is reinforced by the fact that shards of clay vessels from that earlier period were among the findings. On the slope of the hill to the right of the bay, strange buildings with conic or semi-circular roofs stimulate our curiosity. We climb up to that point. They are small, derelict structures consisting of one main area with a single opening as entrance. Many discussions have taken place between archaeologists about these structures, without any certain conclusions being reached. The fact remains that the shape of their roofs and other features can be found in the architecture of the East, which is why it is speculated that this was a settlement of Saracens built between the 8th and 9th centuries AD. This was of course the period in which Saracen pirates were making repeated raids in the Aegean and so it is possible that they may have established a base in the little harbour of Palatia. The only certainty is that this settlement was built on a site where others had existed previously: first, that of ancient Nisyros and later, an early Christian village. Opposite the white beach a mountain looms up like a huge rock that has been split in two. In the gorge created, we are told, by a major earthquake, runs the Entis stream. It is worth walking through the gorge. But before arriving at the entrance, we see a white chapel, with red tiles on its roof and pile of broken marble pieces around it. It is Ayia Sofia, on the site once occupied by a large early Christian basilica in the 5th century. Among the marble pieces that have been preserved from the old church is a capital. We leave this very interesting church and head for the gorge.

1

2   At its entrance are two large caves high in the rock that provide protection from the hot summer sun and from the wind and rain of winter to the sheep and goats who can climb up that high.
On the top of the mountain we can see the chapel of Ayios Zacharias from far below. We follow the upward path between the rocks. To the right and left are the almost vertical sides of the gorge.

After a walk of about 45 minutes, we emerge from the gorge, having reached a clearing in which is the abandoned and half-ruined settlement of Argos. Here there are a number of rural cottages
3   which the local people call «stables», a name similar to the one used for the houses in Avlona near Olympos. Shepherds used to live in these cottages, and beside them, in the same group of buildings, were their sheep and goats. There was also a cistern inside the «stables», in which rainwater was collected from the roofs, to be used when the shepherds were obliged to remain in this house for the winter owing to pirates' raids.

The ancient name of Argos, which is retained to the present day, clearly indicates that this place must have had its own history. Indeed a little pre-
4   historic settlement was discovered there, which yielded findings from the late Neolithic to the Minoan period.

This is the unknown islet of Saria with an area of just 17 km^2 and two or three «occasional» inhabitants, shepherds who may or may not stay there even during the summer. We have already gathered our impressions and must return to Palatia. The little boat is waiting to take us back to Diafani and immediately afterward we return to Pigadia. We say goodbye to unspoiled beauty. It was a real surprise, and it waited until the end of our tour of Karpathos to make its appearance.

Saria: memories of the picturesque past in all its magnificence
1. The buildings on the hill are reminiscent of the East,
*   reminding us that the Saracens once roamed these parts.*
2. Views of Saria with the isolated chapels of Ayios Zacharias.
3. Ayia Sofia.

There is one day in the year, 7th June, when if you are strolling through the narrow streets of Kassos, you'll meet a multitude of visitors, most of whom are Greeks from New York. They have all come on a long trip to the island solely to celebrate, with their few remaining fellow Kassiots, the island's most important anniversary, that of the Holocaust.

A small, rocky island with a long maritime tradition, Kassos has been abandoned by the greater part of its population, who wanted to try their luck in foreign countries, primarily in the US and Egypt (in Egypt they took part in the building of the Suez canal in the mid-19th century). Many Kassiots are today seafarers, mainly captains or shipowners who sail all the seas in the world. The folklore elements that exist on Karpathos can be seen equally intensely on Kassos, the only difference being that on Kassos the influence from nearby Crete is more visible. It can be seen in festivals and other events, when Kassiot songs and dances follow Cretan dances and mantinades. There are just a few villages on Kassos, and very few people; so it is an opportunity for the visitor to get closer to them and to feel their warm hospitality. It is an opportunity to spend tranquil, carefree holidays.

Geography

Kassos is the southernmost island of the Dodecanese and is situated between Karpathos and Crete. It has an area of 66 km²; its coastline is 50 km long, and the number of permanent residents, who are engaged in farming, stock-breeding and fishing, is just over 1100.

The other Hydra

History

We do not know for certain who the first inhabitants of Kassos were. But there are indications that the Achaeans had inhabited the island prior to the Phoenicians. These indications are reinforced by finds in the cave of Ellinokamara and by the fact that a site in the middle of the island is called Argos. The Achaeans and Phoenicians were succeeded by the Dorians and then, along general lines, the island followed the fortunes of the Dodecanese and particular that of neighbouring Karpathos.

But what must be emphasised in particular about Kassos is its tradition at sea and its maritime strength during recent centuries, which could be seen as early as 1779, when the French traveller Savary visited it, and described the island as «a small maritime community that is sustained by shipping and trade, particularly with Syria».

When Greece's War of Revolution against the Turks began in 1821, Kassos contributed 22 three-masted warships to the struggle, and 60 cargo vessels most of which were armed. All these ships cooperated closely with the famous fighters of Hydra and Spetses. The fleet would anchor during the summer on the opposite islet of Armathia and in winter at Tristomo, on Karpathos, and became such a serious annoyance to the Sultan and Ibrahaim Pasha, that after one failure, they succeeded in capturing the island on 7 June 1824.

Very few of the islanders escaped the massacre and the entire island of Kassos was put to the torch. That was the Holocaust, the anniversary of which is commemorated by Kassiots all together every year.

The subsequent history of the island resembles that of the other islands of the Dodecanese. Liberation followed in 1823, then Turkish domination was reinstated by virtue of the Protocol of London in 1830, and the Italian occupation began in 1912. Kassos was united with Greece in 1948.

Fry and its beaches

From the ship, Kassos looks like a mountainous island without deep gullies, but with mountains that look very high for such a small island. **Fry**, its capital and main port, is on its northern coast, in an area that constitutes an exception because it is not mountainous; the terrain simply rises gradually as it approaches the mountain. The ferry is moored at a little wharf, on whose right hand is a breakwater to protect it from the waves. To the left is a tiny, picturesque harbour called **Bouka**, full of fishing boats, always a theme that lends itself to photography. There are a few houses in front of the little port and right afterwards is the church of **Ayios Spyridon**, patron saint of the island. Its roof consists of four semi-circular domes covered by red tiles. Beside it is a fine four-storey bell-tower with a clock. From Bouka, a main street heads toward the centre of the village. On it are most of the shops, restaurants

2, 3. Views of the Kassos harbour.

and coffee shops. It is worth seeing the archaeo-logical collection and the municipal library, as well as some of the captain's mansions or traditional Kassiot houses with their wooden decoration on the interior and all the folkloric elements that we have noted in the Karpathian house.

There is a little beach to the east of Bouka and very close to it; but practically everybody prefers to swim on the beach 500 m. to the west of Fry, or even farther away, on the beaches of Amua (3 km) and Antiperato (4 km) (there is a road that goes to the beach). Farther still there are other secluded beaches among which is Fokiokamara. But the most beautiful sandy beach is on the island of **Armathia** northwest of Fry and about 3 miles from it. During the summer there are daily excursions from Fry.

Apart from the island's official feastday on 7 June, about which we spoke in the introduction, the town of Fry organises various events during the summer, including concerts, theatrical performances and Kassiot evenings with music and local traditional instruments and dancing. Fry's regular festival is celebrated on 12 De-cember, the feast of St Spyridon. The festivities on that date include the contribution of food by the church, as is the case with the other festivals on the island. At Fry there are very few hotels, but quite a few rooms to rent.

1. Village of Ayia Marina.
2. Solitary windmill has become a landmark on the island.
3. Church of the Panayia (Virgin Mary) in the village of Panayia.
4. Church of Ayios Panteleimon.

Tour of the island

After about half a kilometre, the coastal road going eastward from Fry leads to **Emporio**, the island's old port, which was used both for trade and as anchorage for warships. Today it is a small summer village in which the only sight to see is the church of the Panayia, built on the site where there was once an early Christian basilica. Beside it there are ancient marble columns and a baptismal font.

From Fry, another road heads up toward the interior of the island toward Poli. About half a kilometre later, is a fork in the road which leads to the little village of **Panayia**, also a summer centre as its permanent residents number no more than 14. Here, too, there is a church of the Panayia with a noteworthy carved wood icon screen and pebble mosaic floor. Its feastday is 15 August, when one of the largest festivals on the island is held.

If we go back to the crossroads leading to Panayia, and head straight up the road, we will reach the village of **Poli**, which is 2 km. from Fry. This is the former capital of the island, and today has 72 inhabitants. It was built at an altitude of 220 m. and offers a lovely view of Fry and the other villages. On this site there was once an ancient town, the existence of which is demonstrated by the remains of a wall on the neighbouring hill, and the discovery in the same area of pots and grave stelae. The church of Ayia Triada (Holy Trinity) draws our attention because of its blue walls and orange domes. It celebrates its feast day in June with the usual festival.

A road heading southeast starts out from Poli and after a steep 4-km climb, takes us to the monastery of **Ayios Mamas**, that looks out over the other side of the island contemplating the sea from high up. A second festival takes place on 2 September in Poli when the monastery celebrates its feast day.

To the west of Fry and about half a kilometre away is the largest and perhaps prettiest village on the island, *Ayia Marina*, with about 500 inhabitants. It covers a large area and among its houses, around which are the usual flower-adorned courtyards, are many villas and captains' mansions. It has attractive churches among which those of Ayia Marina, Christ Church and Stavros may be singled out. And of course festivals take place in the village on these churches' feast days: the largest perhaps, that of Ayia Marina, is on 17 July, that of Christ Church is on 6 August and the True Cross is on 4 September. Near Ayia Marina is the cave of *Ellinokamara*, noteworthy for both historical and archaeological reasons. The local people sought refuge there during pirate raids but also, as shown by artifacts found in it, it was used as a cult site from the Mycenean to the Hellenistic age. What impresses the visitor is the fact that its entrance is closed by large hewn boulders used in ashlar masonry. There are two openings in the wall.

About 2 km southeast of this cave is a second one, the *Selai* cave, of solely visual interest for its attractive stalactites.

A road that starts out from Fry and crosses the island heading southwest leads, after 2.5 km, to *Arvanitohori* with its 240 inhabitants, many mansions and the lovely church of Ayios Dimitrios, which celebrates its feast day and festival on 26 October. The same road, no longer paved, crosses the Argos site in the centre of the island, and at a distance of 10 km from Fry, takes us to the monastery of Ayios Georgios (feast day 23 April), in Hadies. The festival lasts for two days, as is the case with most of the festivals on the island, and people taking part are offered not only their meals for these days but also accommodation in the monastery's spacious guest houses. The monastery is famous for its religious paintings and carved wood icon screen. From here the road continues, ending 2 km later at the Helandros bay, the southernmost point of Kassos with its best beach.

Karpathos

Kassos

KARPATHOS

How to get to Karpathos

There are from one to five flights a day from Athens to Karpathos according to the season. You can also fly from Rhodes, Kassos and, in summer, from Sitia in Crete. For further information, please call Olympic Airways at (01) 966-6666.

Ferries leave Piraeus (via Crete) two or three times a week according to the season. These routes usually include the following destinations: Piraeus, Milos (Cyclades), Ayios Nikolas (Crete), Sitia (Crete), Kassos, Karpathos and Rhodes. The trip from Piraeus to Karpathos lasts about 19 hours.

For further information please call the Piraeus Port Authority at (01) 422-6000/4 or the agency at (01) 427-4009, 411-0716. One may also call the Hellenic Telecommunications Organisation (OTE) at 143 for information about ships departing from Piraeus in the following 24 hours.

Where to stay

Karpathos has many hotels in the various regions, (Pigadia, Amopi, Arkassa, Diafani, Lefkos, Makris Yialos and Menetes (see hotel chart). It also has more than 35 apartments with hotel facilities (30 of which are in Pigadia) and many rooms to rent or furnished apartments in the regions above, to which we can add Finiki, Kyra-Panayia and Olympos.

Local transportation on Karpathos

Pigadia is connected with all the villages on the island by local bus service. Bus service to Amopi beach is more frequent in summer. For Diafani and Olympos, two small boats leave from Pigadia every morning in the summer and dock in Diafani.

From there, visitors to Olympos are taken to the village by bus, and return the same afternoon to Diafani where they board the boats waiting to take them back to Pigadia. The same boats extend their itineraries from Diafani to Saria twice a week.

Regarding the famous beaches on the east coast, such as Ahata, Kyra-Panayia, Apella and the others, small craft are available to take people on day trips from Pigadia and Diafani.

Useful telephone numbers on Karpathos (0245)

Town Hall 22427
Health Centre 22228
Police 22222
Port Authority 22227
Olympic Airways 22057
Taxi 22705
Post Office 22219
Police, Aperi 31253
Police, Arkassa 61250
Police, Diafani 51213
Police, Mesohori 71210
Community of Olympos 51203

Pigadia (0245)									
ASTRON	B	22774	ROMANTIKA	C	22460	Arkassa (0245)			
VENETIA	B	22008	SUNRISE	C	22467	ARKESIA	B	61290	
ELECTRA BEACH	B	22577	TITANIA	C	22144	DIMITRIOS	B	61313	
MEDITERRANEAN	B	22793	FOTINI BEACH	C	22523	Diafani (0245)			
MIRAMARE BAY	B	22354	HARIS	C	22583	BALASKAS	C	51320	
SEVEN STARS	B	22101	OCEANIS	C	22975	NIKOS	E	51289	
ALEX	C	22004	ANESIS	D	22100	Lefkos (0245)			
APOLLON	C	22800	KARPATHOS	D	22347	KRINOS	C	71410	
ATLANTIS	C	22200	Amopi (0245)			Makris Yialos (0245)			
OLKOS	C	22192	ALBATROSS	B	22828	IRENE	B	22143	
BLUE BAY	C	22479	AMOPIS BAY	C	22184	LONG BEACH	C	23076	
OLYMPIC	C	22708	HELIOS	C	22448	Menetes (0245)			
PANORAMA	C	22739	SOPHIA	C	22078	ARGO	C	22589	
PORPHYRIS	C	22294	Aphiartis (0245)						
			POSEIDON	C	22070				

 KASSOS

How to get to Kassos

You can fly to Kassos from Athens (via Rhodes) at least three times a week. You can also get there from Rhodes, Karpathos and, in summer, from Sitia in Crete. For further information, call Olympic Airways at (01) 966-6666.

There are ferries from Piraeus (via Crete) 2 or 3 times a week depending on the season. The route covered on these trips is usually as follows: Piraeus, Milos (Cyclades), Ayios Nikolas (Crete), Sitia (Crete), Kassos, Karpathos and Rhodes. The trip from Piraeus to Kasssos lasts about 18 hours.

For further information please call the Piraeus Port Authority (01) 422-6000/4 or the agency at (01) 427- 4009, 411-0716. One may also call the Hellenic Telecommunications Organisation (OTE) at 143 for information about ships departing from Piraeus in the following 24 hours.

Where to stay

In Fry there are two hotels: the Anagennisis (3rd class) tel. (0245) 41495 and the Anesis (3rd class) tel. (0245) 41201. There are also rooms and apartments to rent

Local transportation on Kassos

Fry is connected with the villages of Kassos by local bus service. Small caiques make daily trips from Fry to the beaches on Armathia. There are also taxis in Fry.

Useful telephone numbers on Kassos (0245)

Town hall 41277
Rural Clinic 41333
Police 41222
Port 41288
Olympic Airways 41555
Post Office .41255

BIBLIOGRAPHY
(All books in Greek)

Evert, Liza; Apostolatos, Gerasimos; Fotiadi, Pelli; *Fifty Small Greek Islands* (Saria), Asterismos Editions - Liza Evert, Athens.

Georgiou, Georgios, *Karpathiaka*, Vol. I, Piraeus 1958.

Melas, E.M. *Karpathos in the Fight for the Rebirth of the Nation,* Athens 1972.

Minas, Konstandinos; Makris, Manolis. *Olympos and Diafani,* Karpathos, published by the Community of Olympos, Karpathos.

Otheitis, Ioannis, *The Revolution on Karpathos*, 5 October 1944, Athens 1965.

Vassilakis, Vassos, *The History of Karpathos,* Piraeus 1969.

Mesohori, *Karpathos,* Vol. I, Athens 1973.